J. Walter Chochola

HAUNTED
GREECE
AND
ROME

HAUNTED GREECE AND ROME

Ghost Stories

from

Classical Antiquity

D. FELTON

University of Texas Press

AUSTIN

Requests for permission to reproduce material from this work should be sent to
Permissions, University of Texas Press, P.O. Box 7819, Austin, TX 78713-7819.

⊛ The paper used in this publication meets the minimum requirements of
American National Standard for Information Sciences—Permanence of Paper for
Printed Library Materials, ANSI Z39.48-1984.

LIBRARY OF CONGRESS CATALOGING-IN-PUBLICATION DATA

Felton, D., 1964–
　　Haunted Greece and Rome : ghost stories from classical antiquity / D. Felton.
　　　　p.　　cm.
　　Based on author's thesis (Ph.D.)—University of North Carolina.
　　Includes bibliographical references (p.　　) and indexes.
　　ISBN 0-292-72507-8 (cloth : alk. paper. — ISBN 0-292-72508-6 (pbk. : alk.
paper)
　　　1. Classical literature—History and criticism.　　2. Ghosts in literature.
　　3. Ghost stories, Classical—History and criticism.　　4. Literature and folklore—
Greece.　　5. Literature and folklore—Rome.　　6. Ghosts—Greece.
　　7. Ghosts—Rome.　　I. Title.
　　PA3015.G48F45　　1999
　　880'.09—dc21
　　　　　　　　　　　　　　　　　　　　　　　　　　　　　98-39213

To the memory of Albert and Edna Dain

Talking of ghosts, he said, "It is wonderful
that five thousand years have now elapsed
since the creation of the world, and still it
is undecided whether or not there has ever
been an instance of the spirit of any person
appearing after death. All argument is
against it; but all belief is for it."

JAMES BOSWELL
Life of Johnson

The same ignorance makes me so bold as
to deny absolutely the truth of the various
ghost stories, and yet with the common,
though strange, reservation that while I
doubt any one of them, still I have faith
in the whole of them taken together.

IMMANUEL KANT
Dreams of a Spirit-Seer

Should Latin, Greek, and Hebrew fail,
*I know a charm which **must** prevail:*
Take but an ounce of Common Sense,
'Twill scare the Ghosts and drive 'em hence.

Public Advertiser
(LONDON),
5 FEBRUARY 1762

CONTENTS

PREFACE

WHILE I WAS DOING GRADUATE WORK IN CLASSICS AT THE University of North Carolina at Chapel Hill, I was introduced to one of the most famous ghost stories from antiquity, Pliny the Younger's tale of a haunted house at Athens. One of the requirements in the program was a course on Latin composition, and our professor, Larry Stephens, had assigned Pliny's story to illustrate the different uses of the imperfect and perfect tenses in a narrative. I had little talent for Latin composition; with apologies to Dr. Stephens, I must admit that I found the supernatural content of the story far more interesting than the technicalities of Pliny's excellent prose style, and I was soon wondering whether there were many more ghost stories like Pliny's surviving from Greece and Rome. As it turned out, there were a great many ghost stories of all kinds. I wanted to write a dissertation on the topic, but as the amount of available material could easily have filled an encyclopedia, I decided to concentrate only on the haunted-house stories. For this book, the dissertation has been greatly revised and expanded to include other types of haunting as well.

There are still many kinds of ghost story excluded from this study. Some people may be disappointed to find that tales of necromancy, of spirit possession, of trips to the underworld, and of witchcraft are not discussed in any detail in these pages. The ghost of Darius from Aeschylus's *Persians,* invoked by his people after their defeat by the Greeks, is mentioned only in passing. The witch Erictho from Lucan's *Pharsalia,* who compels a corpse to speak in what must be the most gruesome necromantic scene ever written, does not make an appearance here. Nor does the wounded werewolf from Petronius's *Satyricon.* The shades of the dead who inhabit the White Isle, too, are absent. Instead, this book focuses on hauntings, cases of revenants and apparitions that come back from the dead of their own accord, appearing to people of this world in order to warn them of danger, to prophesy, to take revenge, to request proper burial, or simply to comfort the living.

Although this study of ghost stories originated as a dissertation written in fulfillment of a Ph.D. in Classics, in its current form the book is intended to appeal not only to classicists but to a wider audience, including folklorists and students of English literature and, ideally, anyone interested in a good ghost story. To make this book accessible to nonclassicists, I have moved nearly all of the Greek and Latin passages into the notes and have provided my own translations of them for the main text.

I am grateful to many people for their assistance and patience during the writing of this book. I thank my original dissertation committee, particularly Kenneth Reckford and George Houston, for allowing me to write on a folkloric topic and for their careful direction. I owe a particular debt to Bill Hansen, who for years now has been a mentor to me concerning folklore in classical literature. I would also like to thank Adrienne Mayor for bringing many of these ghost stories to my attention, Don Lateiner for spending so much time discussing crisis apparitions with me, and Sylvia Grider for generously allowing me to preview her paper on haunted houses in literature and culture. Jeff Carnes, Dave Johnson, Marybeth Lavrakas, Joan O'Brien, and Lisa Splittgerber read the manuscript at various stages, and I am very grateful for their valuable comments and suggestions. I thank the Center for Hellenic Studies in Washington, D.C., for a fellowship that allowed me the time and resources to concentrate on parts of this book during the summer of 1996. I am particularly grateful for the expert guidance of several people associated with the University of Texas Press, including Ali Hossaini, Jim Burr, Leslie Tingle, and copyeditor Sherry Wert.

Finally, I wish to thank my family and friends, without whose encouragement, support, and patience this book would not have been completed.

INTRODUCTION

THIS IS A BOOK ABOUT HAUNTINGS—HAUNTINGS RECORDED TWO
thousand years ago by the writers of ancient Greece and Rome. Stories of
hauntings and other kinds of ghostly manifestation seem to have been as
popular in antiquity as they are today,[1] and reports of hauntings are found
in many different types of literature surviving from the classical world. They
appear in the epic poetry of Homer and Vergil, the tragedies of Aeschylus
and Seneca, the histories of Herodotus and Tacitus, the geography of Pausanias, the biographies of Plutarch, and many other genres. The comedies
of Plautus, the letters of Pliny the Younger, and the satires of Lucian contain
some of the best-known tales of hauntings from ancient times.

"Haunting" is the repeated manifestation of strange and inexplicable
sensory phenomena—sounds, tactile sensations, smells, and visual hallucinations—generally said to be caused by ghosts or spirits attached to a certain locale.[2] Hauntings are the appearances of ghosts to people who were
not actually trying to summon them, and in this respect hauntings differ
greatly from necromantic ceremonies and *katabaseis,* or trips to the underworld, both of which involve intentional visitation and consultation with
the dead. The term "haunt" is related to the word "home," and typically a
haunted location is the former home of the deceased or the spot where the
deceased died. Haunted sites can also include places that were frequented
or favored by the deceased. But as folklorists and parapsychologists point
out, there is really no general pattern to a haunting. Some phenomena
manifest themselves periodically or continually over time, whereas others
occur only on "anniversary dates," such as the date of death.[3] Though most
hauntings involve apparitions, some involve only noises, such as mysterious
footsteps or groaning. Others are characterized only by curious odors or
chill breezes. And although hauntings are generally distinguished by their
recurrent quality, some types of apparition that appear only once, at a crucial time, are often considered to be hauntings.[4]

Despite the apparent popularity of these tales in antiquity, few studies of ancient ghost stories exist, and little has been written about ghosts as folk-loric or literary figures in antiquity. Because relatively few stories of any length have survived, researchers are left almost no context in which to analyze them. The corpus available for study seems limited, because the longer stories—such as those of Plautus, Pliny, and Lucian—are only a few paragraphs in length, whereas the majority of ghost stories are only a few sentences long.

Another possible reason for the lack of critical attention given to ancient ghost stories is the corresponding lack of classification of supernatural phenomena—how, for example, to distinguish ghost stories from stories dealing with other types of supernatural being. This reflects a certain amount of confusion about how to define what constitutes a "ghost." Nowadays a ghost is often defined as "a disembodied figure believed to be the spirit of a living being who has died,"[5] but in antiquity both the terminology used to describe such beings and the concept of "spirits of the dead" itself were much more generalized. Some ghosts were indeed considered to be the insubstantial spirits of the deceased, but the general title of "ghost" was also applied to all sorts of impersonal semi-divine apparitions, daimones, and other kinds of supernatural being, none of which were considered to be the spirits of people who had died.

This lack of specific categorization is largely due to the ancients' perception of the supernatural. There were often no functional distinctions between the gods and other types of supernatural being, and many phenomena that modern folklore attributes specifically to ghosts were, in antiquity, considered communications from the gods. For example, odd phenomena such as showers of stones, doors opening by themselves, and disembodied voices are nowadays generally classified as poltergeist activity by folklorists and parapsychologists. In antiquity, however, such phenomena were considered portents.[6] That the Greeks and Romans did not divide things up the way we do is reflected in the lack of a distinct vocabulary to describe these phenomena. In Greek, for example, the words δαίμων (*daimōn*) and φάσμα (*phasma*) were used to describe nearly every type of supernatural activity, from gods to ghosts. In Latin as well, there was little distinction. Words such as *monstrum,* used in Roman state religion to refer to prodigies of nature, were also used to describe ghosts, which were usually not considered prodigies. But an examination of various ghost stories from antiquity shows that there were certain folkloric traditions associated with disembodied spirits of the dead, and different traditions associated with other types of supernatural being.

Although there has been little written about hauntings in antiquity, there has been a great deal written about Greek and Roman perceptions of death, the soul, and the afterlife.[7] These studies discuss in depth the various conflicting views of the underworld in antiquity, such as those found in Homer and Vergil.[8] The inconsistencies were nicely expressed by Sir Thomas Browne (1605–1682) in his *Hydriotaphia* ("Urn Burial"):

> The departed spirits know things past and to come, yet are ignorant of things present. *Agamemnon* fortels what should happen unto *Ulysses,* yet ignorantly enquires what is become of his own Son. The Ghosts are afraid of swords in *Homer,* yet *Sibylla* tells *Aeneas* in *Virgil,* the thin habit of spirits was beyond the force of weapons. The spirits put off their malice with their bodies, and *Caesar* and *Pompey* accord in Latine Hell, yet *Ajax* in *Homer* endures not a conference with *Ulysses:* And *Deiphobus* appears all mangled in *Virgils* Ghosts, yet we meet with perfect shadows among the wounded ghosts of *Homer.*[9]

Such inconsistencies in beliefs about the survival of the soul after death were accompanied by a lack of consensus in antiquity as to whether ghosts even existed. Some ancient Greeks claimed to see ghosts, whereas others, such as the Epicureans, were highly skeptical, trying to find material explanations for such phenomena. As Hopkins observes, the Greek and Roman beliefs "ranged from the completely nihilistic denial of after-life, through a vague sense of souls' ghostly existence, to a concept of the individual soul's survival and of personal survival in a recognisable form."[10] Roman beliefs about life after death were extraordinarily varied. No single orthodoxy dominated; polytheism was supplemented by philosophical speculation and by individual sects such as Stoicism, Mithraism, Judaism, and eventually Christianity.[11]

Particular attention has also been paid to ghosts in Greek and Roman drama, where they often motivate the action. Whitmore (1915) presents a general study on the supernatural in tragedy, briefly mentioning the role of the supernatural in classical drama. Klotsche (1918) gathers many examples of supernatural events in the tragedies of Euripides and discusses them in a religious context, and Braginton (1933) does the same for Seneca's tragedies. Probably the most important and thorough study of ghosts in classical drama is Hickman's *Ghostly Etiquette on the Classical Stage* (1938), which examines the function of ghosts as stage characters in Greek and Roman tragedy and comedy, including even the fragmentary plays. The work takes into detailed consideration many well-known stage ghosts, such as Darius in Aeschylus's *Persians,* Polydorus in Euripides' *Hecuba,* and Tantalus in Seneca's *Thyestes.* Also analyzed are references to less familiar ghosts in the remnants of Roman tragedies by Ennius, Pacuvius, and Accius, and possible allusions to ghosts in the fragments of several Greek and Roman comedies. In addition to discussing ghosts that appear onstage in classical drama, Hickman points out the roles of ghosts that are only reported by other characters and never appear onstage. Hickman analyzes many aspects of the ghostly characters, including, for example, their physical appearance and clothing (when described), whether they speak or remain silent, which other characters are able to see them, what their motive is for appearing, and whether any physical phenomena, such as earthquakes or thunder, accompany their appearance. The work concludes with a brief look at ghosts in world drama and how later dramatists imitated the ghostly technique of classical writers.

The ghosts in Greek and Roman tragedy have perhaps had more appeal for scholars because they are dramatic characters with a substantial context for analysis, unlike other ghosts in the extant classical literature, which are mentioned only briefly in short local legends.

Outside of drama, Nardi has done detailed work on the legal aspects of ancient and modern haunted houses, and Radermacher discusses haunted houses briefly in his article on Lucian's supernatural stories and their religious implications.[12] Aside from these studies, however, we have only basic collections of ancient ghost stories with little or no interpretation of them. Such collections include Wendland's "Antike Geister- und Gespensterge-schichten" (1911), which gathers many stories of supernatural phenomena together under various headings; Collison-Morley's *Greek and Roman Ghost Stories* ([1912] 1968), which retells many of the stories from antiquity and provides modern British equivalents; W. M. S. Russell's "Greek and Roman Ghosts" ([1980] 1981), which selects a few stories and places them in a folkloric context; and Kytzler's *Geister, Gräber und Gespenster: Antike Spuk-geschichten* (1989), another collection of Greek and Roman supernatural tales. Other than Russell's essay, none of these studies deals with the ancient ghost stories from a folkloric point of view, and none of them includes literary analysis. But stories of hauntings have been popular for a very long time, and, as Hickman notes, since ghosts have continued in popularity for nearly three thousand years, they surely merit a special study.[13]

Moreover, modern writers of ghost stories are indebted to the Greek and Roman innovations, and it is surprising that classical scholars generally disparage ancient ghost stories. One commentator says, for example, "No one can help being struck by the bald and meagre character of these stories as a whole. They possess few of the qualities we expect to find in a good modern ghost story."[14] Another remarks on the "feebleness of many ancient ghost stories" *when judged by modern standards*.[15] This attitude, I suspect, is partially responsible for the lack of critical attention given to the ancient ghost stories. Aside from the unfairness of judging classical stories by modern standards, these comments show that the ancient ghost stories have not been recognized as being, for the most part, recorded folk legends rather than fully developed literary fiction. Furthermore, the few longer ghost stories that remain, such as those of Pliny and Lucian, influenced the supernatural fiction of many great modern ghost-story writers—an influence that goes largely unrecognized when we dismiss the ancient ghost stories with only superficial analysis.

Though scholars in the field of classics have been slow to acknowledge the importance of ancient ghost stories to later literature, such has not been the case with scholars of English and American literature. Penzoldt, Briggs, and Lovecraft, among others who discuss the development of the modern ghost story, point out the importance of Greek and Roman ghost stories in their opening chapters.[16] And although classicists might not have considered ancient ghost stories from a literary or folkloric point of view, several of them have been interested from a parapsychological standpoint. One of the main classicists to show interest in ghost stories from antiquity was E. R. Dodds, who from his early youth "was actively interested, like his predecessor Gilbert Murray, in psychical research; he served on the council of the Society for Psychical Research from 1927, and was President from 1961 to 1963. He found evidence for telepathy convincing, but though retaining an open mind about the subject he was never persuaded by the alleged evidence for survival after death."[17] Dodds did not find as much evidence in classical literature as he had hoped to, and as Collison-Morley points out, "The Greek and Roman [ghost] stories hardly come up to the standards required by the Society for Psychical Research. They are purely popular. . . . Naturally, they were never submitted to critical inquiry, and there is no foreshadowing of any of the modern theories" about what might cause such phenomena.[18]

This study undertakes to examine stories of hauntings from classical antiquity, giving particular attention to the longer tales of Plautus, Pliny, and Lucian, which center on haunted houses. I do not intend this book to be an exhaustive listing of ghost stories in the extant Greek and Roman literature; rather, I hope to give a representative sampling of the kinds of ghostly phenomena most frequently found therein, providing a folkloric perspective for such an analysis. As Dundes notes, the literary critic without proper knowledge of folklore can go wrong in identification and consequently in interpretation; conversely, too many folklorists, attempting to study literature, do little more than read for motifs without attempting to evaluate how an author uses folkloric elements and how those elements function in the literary work as a whole.[19] By examining classical ghost stories in a folkloric context, we can see the importance of identifying and interpreting the presence of folkloric elements in literature.

The first chapter of this study explains the folkloric context of ghost stories by discussing various beliefs and rituals concerning ghosts in antiquity. Many of the folk-beliefs about ghosts recorded by the Greeks and Romans can still be found today—for example, the beliefs that certain animals are able to detect the presence of ghosts, that certain kinds of ghost tend to appear at midnight and others at midday, and that ghosts vanish at cockcrow. Though these folk-beliefs were widespread in the ancient world, as were various festivals to honor and appease the dead, there was at the same time skepticism expressed about the nature of apparitions, and many scientists and philosophers such as Aristotle and Lucretius tried to find physical explanations for these alleged supernatural events.

The second chapter examines problems in defining and classifying different sorts of ghostly phenomena. Because the Greeks and Romans generally made no specific distinctions between ghosts, semi-divine apparitions, and other daimones, Greek and Latin words for ghosts and other apparitions are generally interchangeable: a word such as *phasma* or *simulacrum* might be applied to the spirit of a dead person appearing in a dream as well as to a minor divinity appearing as a waking vision. This is because all such phenomena were part of "nature" as the Greeks and Romans knew it.[20] Today, folklorists and parapsychologists classify diverse paranormal phenomena, and looking back at the ghost stories from antiquity, we can see that differences existed between the kinds of supernatural phenomena described by the Greek and Roman writers, even if those writers and their societies saw no need to point out such distinctions. The main types of ghost involved in hauntings include revenants (or "embodied ghosts"), warning apparitions, poltergeists, and "continual" apparitions.

Evidently the most popular of the ghost stories were those concerning haunted houses, which are the focus of the third chapter in this book. From the few haunted-house stories surviving from classical times, it is possible to extract a basic narrative structure, as well as to examine details of the stories in the folkloric context already established. Of particular interest are the realistic details that often appear in such stories, for example, specifics regarding the difficulty in selling or renting out a haunted property. From accounts of haunted houses in antiquity, we can see that disclosure laws regarding haunted property have not changed much in two thousand years.

Chapters 4, 5, and 6 of this study examine in detail some of the best-known stories of hauntings that survive from antiquity: the haunted-house story from the *Mostellaria* by the comic playwright Plautus; the ghost stories from the letters of Pliny the Younger, including his famous account of a haunted house at Athens; and the supernatural tales from the dialogue *Philopseudes* of the satirist Lucian. The works of these authors are particularly significant because we can see in them a development toward the ghost story as a work of literary fiction rather than the ghost story as recorded folk-legend.

We should not ignore the influence of these ancient stories on the modern literary ghost-story tradition. The stories from Greece and Rome had a strong effect on the nineteenth- and twentieth-century writers of ghost stories, and the last chapter in this book looks at some specific examples of this. As Dorothy Scarborough wryly observed in explaining the lasting appeal of ghost stories, the appearance of ghosts "has always elicited considerable interest on the part of humanity. Their substance of materialization, their bearing, dress, and general demeanor are matters of definite concern to those who expect shortly to become ghosts themselves."[21]

HAUNTED
GREECE
AND
ROME

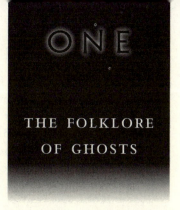

ONE

THE FOLKLORE
OF GHOSTS

THE GREEKS AND ROMANS HAD NO CONCEPT OR ENCOMPASSING term for folklore as such, although they did recognize and have names for many of the traditional forms of expression now classified as genres of folklore.[1] Folklore, generally defined as the traditional beliefs, practices, and tales of a people, subsists mainly on oral tradition, with the key word being "tradition." Folklore is characterized by various units of traditional material that are memorable and consequently repeatable, and "tradition" is the main idea that links together the many subtypes we can distinguish within the field of folklore, such as proverbs, riddles, ballads, greeting and leave-taking formulas, anecdotes, jokes, tall tales, tongue-twisters, and other categories under the heading of verbal art.[2] Under this heading we also find the several areas of folklore with which classicists may be the most familiar: folktales, myths, and legends,[3] three areas generally classified as narratives, to distinguish them from other types of verbal art, such as proverbs and riddles.[4]

Though these three categories can overlap to a certain extent, they do have specific characteristics that allow us to distinguish among them. Bascom, summarizing many decades of discussion on this issue, explains the difference as follows.[5] Folktales, also known by the German term *Märchen,* are narratives regarded as pure fiction; they have conventional openings, such as "Once upon a time, in a land far, far away," which usually fix the story as timeless and placeless; and the principal characters may be human or nonhuman. The various subgenres of folktales include fables, animal tales, and trickster tales. Myths, on the other hand, are narratives considered to be truthful accounts of what happened in the remote past; in many cultures they are sacred, and usually associated with theology and ritual. Their main characters are often not human beings, but may have human attributes; they are deities or culture heroes, for example, whose actions are set in an earlier time, when the earth was different from what it is today. Myths are often etiological, accounting for the origin of the world and everything in it. Legends, finally, are narratives that, like myths, may be regarded as true by the narrator and his audience, but are set in a period considered less remote, when the world was much as it is today. Characters in legends are mainly human, and the stories are more secular than sacred, though some legends have developed around saints. Most legends are long stories of wars, kings, and successions; but legends also include local tales about such diverse subjects as buried treasure and ghosts.

It is important to realize, however, that "slippage" between such narrative classifications is widely recognized among scholars, and classifying folk narratives can be a very complex matter. The modern ghost story, partially because of its literary ancestry, may be more closely related to the folktale than to the legend.[6] But Greek and Roman ghost stories, particularly as transmitters of folk-belief, generally fit into the category of legends. Ghosts appearing as characters in drama tend to be exceptions, as such characters are not always based on legend but are created as dramatic devices. The haunted-house episode from Plautus's *Mostellaria* is a better example of a ghost story in drama based on legend, which becomes evident when we compare the episode to other haunted-house stories from antiquity. Plautus's version is not a prose narrative, but it is a literary, or dramatic, adaptation of a common type of legend circulating in society, and we find in it the same narrative structure that exists in other such stories.[7] What the ghost stories have in common as legends is that to a certain extent they are believed, or believable, within the segments of the societies in which they occur; they are set in the real world, in the recent past; and they involve normal human beings rather than ancient gods or heroes in the roles of protagonists.[8] For legends in general, a major function has always been the attempt to explain unusual and supernatural happenings in the natural world,[9] which is why ghost stories fall easily into this category.

Many local legends nowadays are often referred to as "migratory legends" or "urban legends," though the label "urban" no longer retains the meaning "associated with the city."[10] What many urban legends have in common is a certain amount of realism. They often concern recent events (or at least alleged events) with an ironic or supernatural component, and there is usually little or no geographical or generational gap between the teller and the event.[11] Urban legends may be told seriously or humorously, circulating, like most folklore, by word of mouth; they are generally anonymous and vary constantly in particular details from one telling to the next, while preserving a central core of traditional elements or "motifs."[12] The stories may be told both in the course of casual conversation and, nowadays, in such special situations as campfires, slumber parties, and college dormitory parties. The stories often contain a phrase such as "this happened to a friend of a friend" (usually referred to as the FOAF),[13] and they are frequently told by a person of some education. The timing and order of events may betray an awareness of literary form, and many times the stories are told by people who do not, generally speaking, accept the supernatural without some skepticism.[14]

Many of these characteristics are found in the Greek and Roman ghost stories, though with fewer specific details about the transmission. Pliny, for example, says simply that he heard his haunted-house story; he does not say where or when. The stories found in Lucian's *Philopseudes* are told as part of a gathering around a companion's sickbed. Plutarch, relating a local legend about haunted baths at Chaeronea, explains that the story has been passed down through generations ("as our ancestors tell us," ὡς οἱ πατέρες ἡμῶν λέγουσι, *Cim.* 1.6). The legends are often set close by, in real physical locations, which sometimes even have reputations for such happenings.[15]

The problem in identifying legends lies in distinguishing the purest forms of orally transmitted tales (e.g., those collected on tape recorders) from literary retellings. But most orally transmitted tales that we have (including, for example, epic) exist because they were in fact written down at some point. The tales, circulated orally, are eventually taken up by minstrels and wandering storytellers, and finally coalesce in the writings of a single mind. Thus "proportion, language, and treatment distinguish a literary folk narrative from the oral folk tale," but both will embody the consciousness and character of the folk from whom the tales arise.[16] This distinction will be important when dealing with Plautus, Pliny, and Lucian, because their ghost stories are literary adaptations of stories that had been circulating in society. Even so, we are able to identify the basic elements (motifs) and other characteristics that point to the stories' origins in oral tradition.

Something many folklorists discuss is the high concentration of humor found in legends of the supernatural, which is true of many ghost stories from antiquity as well as more modern supernatural stories. In Plautus and Lucian, not surprisingly, the comic elements predominate over the terror of the supernatural, and even Pliny, who cannot be said to have had much of a sense of humor, includes at least one comic moment in his haunted-house story—whether intentionally or not. The presence of humor is somewhat unexpected in stories about death and unhappy spirits. But the Solomons suggest:

> In many respects [the supernatural and the humorous] . . . are fraternal twins. Both serve to entertain, both depend on exaggeration, distortion,

or some unusual or magnified quality. . . . A thread of comedy may appear in the most terrifying tale of terror, and the existence of a great body of jokes, anecdotes, and folk pranks about the supernatural confirms the common root of humorous and supernatural folk tales.[17]

Also, both the supernatural and the humorous provide a catharsis through the recognition of certain experiences common to all folk.[18] In the case of the supernatural, the humor provides a way of dealing with the disturbing reality of death. Halpert makes a similar connection as he explains the difficulty of classifying folktales and legends as *either* supernatural *or* humorous:

> We must be prepared to find in many extremely serious areas of belief, custom, and legend, such as death and burial and ghostlore, a proliferation of humorous explanatory stories and mocking anecdotes that seem to deny the seriousness of these very serious subjects. . . . Many humorous stories of deathbed requests for burial in a certain way also reflected at least the past existence of serious concern with the way in which the dead were interred. I suggest that such juxtapositions occur particularly on topics that are emotionally charged and that the humorous tales cannot be arbitrarily separated from the serious areas, in classification, without disturbing the significance of these very complex patterns.[19]

There can also be significant differences between the supernatural and the humorous: tales of the supernatural tend to leave more room for belief than exaggerated humorous tall tales.[20] While the particulars of any given supernatural tale may be doubted, few people entirely exclude the possibility of supernatural occurrences, and just about everybody is curious about death.[21]

In addition to identifying ghost stories themselves as a type of folklore (narrative), several other aspects of ghost-lore need to be recognized. The stories contain much information about superstitions concerning ghosts, the interdependence of folklore and religion, and the tension between religion and skepticism regarding the nature of ghosts and the existence of the soul. Identifying such elements in the ghost stories adds to our picture of Greek and Roman beliefs.

Folk-Beliefs Concerning Ghosts

The Greeks and Romans had many folk-beliefs concerning ghosts. A comprehensive listing would fill an encyclopedia; it will suffice here to look at several of the more popular beliefs. Some are very specific, whereas others are broader in scope; many still exist in some form today, but others have disappeared from society. Pliny the Elder, for example, mentions in several places in his *Natural History* that spirits would not approach people who had freckles, which were considered a kind of stain that needed to be removed. People with freckles were somehow considered polluted with regard to religious matters, and they were not allowed to assist at magic rituals, as that would keep spirits away.[22] According to Pliny, spirits would not obey people with freckles, and also could not be seen by such people.[23]

The fourth-century Greek author Theophrastus, in his *Characters,* describes the typical "superstitious" man or *deisidaimōn* (δεισιδαίμων, from the Greek δεισιδαιμονία; literally, "fear of spiritual things"). Theophrastus exaggerates the characteristics of superstitious people to satirize them, and the character of the *deisidaimōn* was one of the stock social types that appeared in Greek New Comedy and its Latin imitators. But Theophrastus, who defines superstition as "cowardice in regard to the supernatural,"[24] based the character on popular folk-beliefs. The superstitious man will not tread upon a tombstone, for fear that association with the dead will pollute him. Likewise, he will not enter a house in which a corpse lies awaiting burial. But he will anoint the stones at crossroads, possibly to appease the ghosts that were thought to gather there. Although there is no direct statement in Greek or Roman literature that ghosts gathered at crossroads, evidence such as this passage from Theophrastus strongly suggests such a belief was present, largely because of the connection between ghosts and Hekate, a nocturnal goddess associated with the dead in the underworld, who was known to frequent crossroads.[25]

There is also evidence for a folk-belief that iron would protect against ghosts.[26] Lucian suggests that ghosts are afraid of the noise of bronze or iron clashing (*Philops.* 15). The tenth Declamation ascribed to Quintilian describes a ghost that is confined to its tomb by means of enchanted iron bars,[27] and the inhabitants of Orchomenos are able to stop a dangerous ghost by burying its bones, making a bronze statue of it, and fastening the statue to a rock with iron (Paus. 9.38.5). The act of binding the statue with iron seems to be a type of sympathetic magic, similar to the use of voodoo dolls.[28] Pliny the Younger, in letter 7.27, describes a ghost that rattles iron chains as if they were a symbol of the ghost's being trapped in limbo between this world and the next.

The belief that ghosts haunt crossroads, along with other more general traditional beliefs, also exists today, though there is no evidence for a direct line of transmission.[29] The belief that dogs have the ability to see ghosts, for example, remains enormously popular.[30] Belief in animal sensitivity to the supernatural was in evidence as early as the *Odyssey,* where Eumaios's dogs

recognize the presence of the disguised Athena and back away whimper-
ing (16.155–63). As Gaster notes, "The belief that animals can descry spirits
is virtually universal."[31] At Theocritus 2.35, dogs howl when Hekate approaches the crossroads, and the elder Pliny says that certain dogs can see
fauns, though men cannot (*HN* 8.40.62). In Lucian, dogs bark prior to the
dramatic appearance of Hekate, and a dog's barking drives away his mis-
tress's ghost (*Philops.* 22–23, 27). Dogs were not the only animals in antiquity believed to be able to sense the presence of spirit beings; horses, too,
seemed to have a "sixth sense." Pausanias records that in the racecourse of
Olympia, horses shied away from an altar; the reason was the proximity of
the tomb of a hero whose ghost frightened the animals (6.20.15–16). Although there are occasional instances of animals other than dogs and horses
sensing ghosts, it is most often these two highly domesticated animals that
are credited with the spirit-seeing ability. It may be these animals' keen
sense of smell rather than sight that lies at the bottom of such traditional
beliefs.[32] Dogs were believed to be able to smell death, and they also have a
connection with corpses, being described frequently in classical literature
as corpse-eaters, as in the opening lines of the *Iliad:* "Sing, goddess, the
wrath of Peleus's son Achilles . . . which sent many brave souls of heroes
down to Hades, but left their bodies as prey for dogs and birds."[33] The
goddess Hekate was often accompanied by dogs.

Another traditional belief found today that also existed in antiquity holds
that ghosts usually appear at midnight, but rarely appear during the day.[34]
This tradition helps us distinguish between ghosts and the so-called warning apparitions discussed in Chapter 2. The latter often appear at midday,
as in the experience of Curtius Rufus described by both Pliny the Younger
and Tacitus: "He was walking in the portico at midday" (*inclinato die spatiabatur in porticu,* Pliny 7.27.2); "At midday he was passing the time alone
in the portico" (*per medium diei porticibus secretus agitat,* Tac. *Ann.* 11.21).[35]
In Lucian, too, the apparition of a giant woman—who turns out to be
Hekate—appears at midday (μεσούσης ἡμέρας, *Philops.* 22).[36] A few
ghosts other than warning apparitions also appear at midday. Phlegon of
Tralles, in his *Mirabilia* 3.4, says the ghost of Bouplagos appears at noon. In
Apuleius's *Metamorphoses* (9.29–30), an extremely unpleasant ghost appears
at midday: First we are told that a jilted wife has arranged for the ghost to
murder her husband. In the next scene, a mysterious woman appears ("At
about midday there appeared suddenly at the mill an ugly woman in the sad
and strange state of an accused criminal," *diem ferme circa mediam repente intra
pistrinum mulier reatu miraque tristitie deformis apparuit,* 9.30). She leads the
husband into his room. When his servants come looking for him, they have

to break down his door, which is locked from the inside. The mysterious woman is nowhere to be seen, but the man is found dead, hanging from a beam. One difference between this case and cases in which the ghosts appear at night is that although we, the audience, know the woman is a ghost, the characters in the story do not realize this until too late.[37]

The majority of ghosts in Greek and Roman stories appear in the dead of night. The ghost stories told to frighten children, which Plato mentions in disapproval, are set at night (*Rep.* 2.381e). In general, night is the time of terrors throughout ancient belief.[38] Ghosts in the haunted-house stories of Pliny and Lucian appear in the middle of the night. Simply put, ghosts belong to the night because nighttime is dark, and darkness is associated with death. Also important is the connection between night and dreams, as many of the ghosts in Greek and Roman stories appear to people at night during their dreams.[39] Related to the belief that ghosts appear at midnight is the belief ghosts will vanish at cockcrow. Philostratus, in his *Life of Apollonius of Tyana* (4.16), describes how Apollonius calls up the ghost of Achilles (accompanied by an earthquake), which vanishes with a flash of lightning, because the cocks were beginning to crow.

One folk-belief current in many countries holds that ghosts will not speak until they are spoken to.[40] There is also a long literary tradition behind this belief. In many stories, a person is pestered by an apparition night after night until it occurs to the sufferer to open a conversation by saying something like, "In the Name of God, why troublest thou me?" At once the ghost is able to speak and explain its predicament: who it is, and what it needs from the living.[41] In Shakespeare's *Hamlet,* for example, when the guards tell Horatio to speak to the ghost of Hamlet's father, they assume that it wishes to communicate but is unable to until someone finds enough courage to speak to it: "Thou art a scholar; speak to it, Horatio" (1.1.45).[42] Another popular example is an anecdote from Boswell on Dr. Johnson, who often sat silently wrapped in thought for a long time. He was once chided by a friend: "Sir (said he), you are like a ghost: you never speak till you are spoken to."[43]

There is some evidence that such a belief may have existed in antiquity. In the extant Greek and Roman ghost stories, certain kinds of ghost are more likely to speak than others. Revenants, which retain their bodies, can speak. Warning apparitions nearly always appear specifically for that purpose, though we shall see a few examples of warning apparitions that communicate through figurative action rather than speech. Ghosts summoned through necromantic ceremonies are intended to speak, as the ghost of Darius does at Aeschylus *Persians* 681ff., the ghost of Melissa in Herodotus

5.92, and the ghost in the gruesome necromantic scene in Lucan 6.413 – 830. Ghosts in dreams, too, appear specifically to speak to the living, such as the ghost of Patroclus, which appears to Achilles in *Iliad* 23.64ff., and the ghost of the murdered Tlepolemus in Apuleius *Metamorphoses* 8.8. But some ghosts in Greek and Roman literature are striking for their lack of speech. The ghost described by Pliny the Younger in letter 7.27 apparently cannot speak, and communicates through gestures with a philosopher who does not attempt to speak with it. Likewise, the ghost in Lucian's haunted-house story at *Philopseudes* 30ff. does not speak, but only attacks the man who confronts it. Plutarch (*Brut.* 36.3 – 4) describes how Brutus bravely faced a ghost. He was sitting in his tent, lost in contemplation, when he thought he heard someone enter. Looking around toward the entrance, he saw a strange and terrible apparition, of unnatural and fearful form, standing near him in silence. Mustering his courage, Brutus asked, "Who are you—are you man or god, and what do you want with me?" The phantom replied, "I am your own evil spirit, Brutus; you shall see me at Philippi."[44] There may be an early origin for the tradition of nonspeaking ghosts: in the underworld scene from *Odyssey* 11, the shades of the dead cannot speak until they drink the sacrificial blood, the substance of life.[45]

Why the Dead Return

In modern ghost-lore, we find many reasons why the dead return. Sometimes they come back to reenact their own deaths, or to reengage in what were their normal pursuits in life. These circumstances result in the "recording" type of haunting discussed in Chapter 2. Some spirits return to complete unfinished business, which may include pointing out to surviving family or friends the location of a missing will, or of a hidden treasure. Some return to punish or take revenge, or to warn the living. Some come back to reward or comfort the living.[46] And in a great many cases, the dead return to request proper burial. In the surviving literature from antiquity, we find several examples from these categories.

Revenge and warning are popular reasons for the dead to return. At Livy 3.58.11, the ghost of the slain Verginia roams from house to house and never rests until all the people involved in her death are brought to justice. At *Aeneid* 1.353 – 57, the murdered Sychaeus appears to Dido in her sleep to say that her brother Pygmalion was the one who killed him, and he warns her to flee: "There came to her as she slept the image of her unburied husband, raising his pale face to her strangely . . . he revealed the whole dark crime of the house. He persuaded her then to flee quickly and leave the country."[47] At Apuleius *Metamorphoses* 9.29–30, a jilted wife arranges for a ghost to kill her husband, as we have seen; at 9.31, the ghost of the murdered husband appears to his daughter in her sleep and reveals that his wife, the girl's stepmother, arranged his murder. Likewise, at *Metamorphoses* 8.8, the ghost of the murdered Tlepolemus comes to his wife in her sleep to warn her against the murderer: "Do not place yourself in the polluted hands of Thrasyllus, nor converse with him, nor recline at his table, nor yield to his bed. Flee the bloody hand of my murderer!"[48]

The most benign ghosts are those which return to comfort or reward the living. In the tenth Declamation ascribed to Quintilian, the ghost of a son appears to his mother simply to comfort her in her grief. After his cremation, he appears to his mother each evening and talks with her until dawn. Unfortunately, the father, upon finding this out, is afraid and calls in a magician to imprison the ghost in its tomb with iron bars. The son stops visiting his mother, who sues the father for willful damage. Also benign are the "Grateful Dead," spirits who return to reward the living who have somehow helped them. The most complete story of this type from antiquity is found in Cicero *De divinatione* 1.27, in a discussion of precognitive dreams:

> [The poet] Simonides, having seen the body of an unknown man lying unburied, buried him. He then planned to go on a sea voyage, but was warned not to go by a vision of the man whom he had buried. The vision told him that if he were to go on the sea voyage, he would perish in a shipwreck. And so Simonides did not go, but those who sailed perished.[49]

Too bad Simonides did not warn the other passengers. The Grateful Dead theme was also expressed by the Hellenistic poet Leonidas of Tarentum, in an epitaph (*Anth. Pal.* 7.657.11–12): "There are, among the dead, those who return favors. . . ."[50] Such stories reflect the widespread concern among Greeks and Romans regarding proper burial rites.

In the majority of cases in antiquity where the disembodied dead return to haunt the living, the motivation is the need for a proper burial. The ghost of Patroclus implies that once the proper funeral rights are performed for his body, he will not haunt the living any longer: "For I will not come again out of Hades, when you have granted me the right of funeral fire" (οὐ γὰρ ἔτ' αὖτις / νίσομαι ἐξ ᾿Αίδαο, ἐπήν με πυρὸς λελάχητε, *Il.* 23.75–76). Elpenor complains to Odysseus that he cannot enter Hades until his body is buried (*Od.* 11.52). As Cumont explains: "From the most ancient time the belief reigned among all the peoples of antiquity that the souls of those who are deprived of burial find no rest in the other life. . . . The fact that the dead had been buried did not suffice; their burial must also have been performed according to the traditional rites." [51] The denial of interment was thought to be the source of infinite torment for the dead, and to throw earth on abandoned corpses was a pious duty. Rohde comments similarly, "The first duty that the survivors owe to their dead is to bury the body in the customary manner. . . . Religious requirements, however, go beyond the law," and it is no mere sanitary regulation to bury the dead.[52] Thus it is the "unwritten laws" of religion that are obeyed by Antigone when she covers the dead body of her brother with a little dust; even such symbolic burial is enough to avert the abomination of improper burial. The fundamental idea underlying all such practices was the one already met with in the *Iliad:* that the soul of the unburied person can find no rest in the hereafter.[53] It is not surprising that the ancients attached the highest importance to the duty of burying the dead, and that Pausanias blames Lysander for not burying the bodies of Philocles and the four thousand slain at Aegospotami, seeing that the Athenians buried even the Persian dead after Marathon (9.32).[54]

The dead do not always request proper rites as politely as Patroclus and Elpenor did. Pausanias tells the story of the ghost of Temesa, who, in anger at the lack of any funeral ceremony, went around killing people and had to be appeased (6.6.7–11). And although *lack* of burial is without question one of the main reasons ghosts haunt this world, *improper* burial or insufficient rites can also bring spirits back. After Achilles was shot by Paris, for example, his ashes were mixed in an urn with those of Patroclus. But Achilles's spirit was not at rest. When the Greeks, having taken Troy, were preparing to sail home, the ghost of Achilles appeared and restrained the troops, because they were departing without leaving any offering on his tomb. Achilles's ghost demanded the sacrifice of Priam's daughter Polyxena. When the Greeks cut her throat over Achilles's tomb, his ghost was appeased.[55] Improper burial caused particularly unpleasant problems upon the death of the emperor Caligula:

> His corpse was carried secretly to the Lamian gardens and, after being only partially burned in a hastily thrown together fire, was buried under a bit of turf. Afterwards it was dug up, cremated, and buried by his sisters when they returned from exile. It is generally agreed that before this was done, the guardians of the gardens were harassed by ghosts; and in that same house where Caligula had been laid out, no night passed without some terror, until the house itself was consumed by fire.[56]

It is clear from folklore and religion that the single most important disturbing factor connected to the appearance of ghosts "is a death without the proper ceremonies. Graves are of importance in most communities. . . . Graves and burials arouse the most powerful emotions." [57] The importance of being buried properly and of resting undisturbed in the grave is reflected in the many curses and legends of curses surrounding the disturbance of certain graves; excavation of Egyptian tombs, for example, gave rise to beliefs about curses on the excavations. [58] The ancient Greeks, particularly those of Asia Minor, wrote imprecations on gravestones warning any potential wrongdoer that evil would befall him if he violated the grave, [59] and some *defixiones* also invoked dire consequences for anyone who might disturb the burial site. [60] Lattimore records a very early example in this seventh-century B.C. epitaph from Rhodes: "I, Idameneus, built this tomb to (my own) glory. May Zeus utterly destroy anyone who disturbs it." [61]

There are psychological reasons for the emphasis placed on burial: the ceremony helps the living sever emotional ties or associations with the recently dead. Relatives and friends may still visit the burial site, but the rite of passage carries with it a certain sense of finality. [62] The idea of *rites de passage,* introduced by Arnold van Gennep in 1909, suggests that death and the land of the dead signify a new state into which a person moves, in principle in the same manner as during his lifetime he moves from one period or position to another (childhood, marriage, fatherhood, for example). In the case of ceremonies for the dying and the dead, the central theme is the joining of the dead person to the departed, and the reorganization of the surviving community. In death ceremonies, the rites of transition and incorporation are more important than the rites of separation. [63]

Suetonius provides us with several extreme examples of what ensues when the living cannot break their emotional links with the dead. These examples are particularly noteworthy: Roman emperors who were responsible for the deaths of their family members, political rivals, and others, and are consequently riddled with guilt. Although Agrippina, who had been murdered by her son Nero, had been buried with due ceremony, Nero's guilty conscience led him to imagine that his mother's ghost was hounding him. He even had rites performed by the Magi, in an effort to summon her shade and ask her forgiveness: "He often confessed that he was harassed by his mother's ghost and by the Furies with whips and burning torches. And so he tried to have Persian magicians conjure up the ghost and beg its forgiveness" (Suet. *Ner.* 34). [64] Agrippina had died a violent death, and Nero could well imagine that she was not resting easy in her grave, though no doubt Nero with his dramatic bent also fancied himself another Orestes. [65]

Otho, after assassinating Galba, had nightmares about the murdered man and tried to propitiate his ghost: "Otho is said to have been terrified that night by Galba's ghost in a terrible nightmare; the servants who ran in when he screamed for help found him lying on the bedroom floor. After this he did everything in his power to placate the ghost" (Suet. *Otho* 7).[66] Likewise the emperor Caracalla, who had murdered his brother, saw phantoms and thought he was being pursued by the ghosts of his father and brother, who were armed with swords (Dio Cass. 78.15).[67] Plutarch records a story told by many people about how the Spartan Pausanias was haunted by the ghost of a Byzantine girl, Cleonice. He had summoned her to his bedroom, but when she approached in the dark, she tripped, and Pausanias, thinking it was an intruder, fatally stabbed her. She kept coming to him in his sleep in phantom form and berating him angrily. After being harassed by the phantom for some time, he went to an oracle and summoned the spirit of Cleonice, asking her to give up her anger. She cryptically replied that his troubles would soon end when he came to Sparta, a reply that seemed to hint at his impending death (*Cim.* 6.4–6).[68]

Festivals for the Dead

The strong belief in the necessity for proper burials and proper rites to accompany them gave rise to certain religious customs concerning the continual appeasement of both those who had already been properly buried and those who had not received the due rites. Families regularly tended the graves of individuals, and in both Greece and Rome, there were special festivals for the dead celebrated by a community as a whole. The Athenians, for example, on the fifth of Boedromion (toward the end of September) celebrated the Genesia, a festival at which the whole citizen body honored the souls of the dead.[69] But the chief festival of all the dead at Athens occurred during the last few days of the Dionysiac feast of the Anthesteria (February–March). It was said that during these days, the ghosts of the dead emerged from the underworld and entered the city, and stayed until they were chased away at the end of the festival.[70] The days were unlucky; temples were closed, and business was suspended. As protection against the ghosts invisibly present, the citizens employed various precautionary measures: they smeared their doors with pitch and chewed hawthorn leaves, and each family made its own offerings to the dead.[71] A meal of mixed grains was cooked and offered to chthonic Hermes for the sake of the dead. At sunset, the master of the house went through the rooms shouting, "Away, Spirits; Anthesteria is over" (θύραζε Κῆρες, οὐκ ἔτ' Ἀνθεστήρια).[72]

Ovid in his *Fasti* describes the Roman festivals in honor of the dead. The two main festivals were the Parentalia and the Lemuria. The Parentalia refers to a period that began on February 13 and lasted ten or eleven days. During these days, magistrates went about in plain clothes, the temples were shut, no fires burned on the altars, and no marriages were contracted. The main day for commemoration of the dead, February 21, was called the Feralia. The general name for the entire period, the Parentalia, indicates that this was a period to commemorate dead kinfolk, though the rites of the Parentalia were observed at the gravesite and not in the house,[73] as Ovid describes in *Fasti* 2.533ff., explaining, "Appease the souls of your ancestors / bring small gifts to the burnt-out pyres" (*animas placate paternas / parvaque in extinctas munera ferte pyras*).

Ovid also describes the Lemuria, or Lemuralia, which took place over three days, May 9, 11, and 13. In a dubious etymology, Ovid derives the name of the festival from Remus, whose gory ghost appeared one day and requested a festival in his honor (*Fast.* 5.451–80). The Lemuria was another festival for bringing offerings to the ghosts of ancestors, but this one took place in the home instead of at the tomb, as the ghosts were thought to return to their old homes for the days of this festival. The ritual involved the head of the family walking through the house with bare feet at dead of night, making the mystic sign with his first and fourth fingers extended, with the other fingers turned inward and the thumb crossed over them (5.433): this was in case he bumped into a ghost as he moved. After washing his hands, he threw black beans over his shoulders, saying, "With these beans I buy back myself and my family" (*his . . . redimo meque meosque fabis,* 5.438). He would say this nine times without looking back, and the ghost was thought to have followed and picked up the beans. Then the master of the house washed again and clashed bronze, and asked the ghost to leave. When he repeated nine times, "Spirits of my ancestors, depart!" (*Manes exite paterni,* 5.443), he looked around; the ceremony was over, and the ghosts had been duly laid to rest for a year.[74]

Another periodic ceremony for the dead observed by Romans was the opening of the *mundus*. This ritual was associated with the spirits of the town dead generally rather than observed by individual families for their family ancestors. When any Roman town was founded, it seems to have been standard practice to dig a trench, called the *mundus,* and throw offerings into it in order to invite the gods to watch over the place and its inhabitants. The trench was then covered with a stone, which came to be thought of as the opening to Hades, as the *mundus* apparently evolved into some sort of subterranean chamber dedicated to underworld spirits. Three times a year (August 24, October 5, and November 8), the stone covering was raised so that these spirits, the *manes,* could emerge and roam the town. The day was holy, and business came to a halt as the ghosts took over the town. No battles could be fought, no ships could set sail, no marriages could take place.[75] But the *manes* also roamed the town during the Parentalia and Lemuria, when the *mundus* was closed, and so the original idea behind the opening of the *mundus* remains unclear.

One aspect of Greek and Roman funerary practice seems to be related to a folk belief that ghosts, which inhabit a shadowy realm, are attracted to lamplight. The goddess Hekate, patron deity of ghosts, was often represented carrying torches to help light the way in the gloomy underworld. In the funerals of ancient Greece, the procession carried torches, symbolically lighting the way to the world to come. Where cremation was practiced, the torches were also used for kindling the pyre. In the process of inhumation, we have no way of knowing what became of the torches—whether they were taken away again, or thrown into the grave. But lamps, commonly found in tombs, suggest the association of fire with inhumation as well as cremation. The practice of putting lamps in graves increased in frequency in Greece beginning in the fifth century B.C.—that is, during the period of increasing preference for cremation.[76] The Romans, too, left lamps at tombs, possibly to represent the eternal spirit. Frazer cites an inscription by a man who stipulated that, in addition to sacrificing on his tomb four times a year in his memory, on the Kalends, Nones, and Ides of every month a burning lamp was to be left on his tomb.[77]

Descriptions of Ghosts in Antiquity

The most thorough treatment so far of descriptions of ghosts in antiquity has been done by Jack Winkler in his article "Lollianos and the Desperadoes." He observes that descriptions of ghosts in antiquity conform to no rigid system, partially because the appearance of a ghost depended on the storyteller's intent and the extent to which he wanted to evoke terror or pity from his audience. Winkler discusses three of the more common appearances of ghosts: pure black, pure white, and smokelike.[78] But many a ghost appeared looking just as the person did in life, or sometimes, if a person's death was particularly gory, his ghost was correspondingly gruesome.

Pausanias (6.6.7–11), describing a picture representing the story of the ghost of Temesa, says that in the picture the daimon was black. The ghost in Lucian's haunted-house story is also pitch-black, and Phlegon of Tralles describes a ghost that appears wearing black clothing (*Mir.* 2.5–6). When the emperor Domitian wanted to terrorize his more important subjects, he used to invite them to dinner in a room decorated in black and entertain them with dances by slave-boys painted black like ghosts (Dio Cass. 67.9). When the philosopher Democritus spent several nights in a tomb, either for peace and quiet or possibly for the purpose of psychical research,[79] some young men dressed up as black-robed skeletons and danced around him, pretending to be ghosts. Unperturbed, he told them to stop being silly (Lucian *Philops.* 32).

Although these last two are masquerades rather than actual reports of ghosts, they do indicate that a belief in black ghosts was common and that such ghosts were supposed to be particularly terrifying. Winkler connects the black color with the gloominess of the underworld, and with nighttime, when many ghosts appear.[80] Russell, also noting the frequent descriptions of ghosts as black, adds that anthropological studies suggest that the way people think of the dead can depend on the way they dispose of them. The Greeks and Romans often burned their dead on pyres in the open air, and consequently last saw them as charred, blackened remains. Most ordinary people were buried without being burned, but the more prestigious and conspicuous funerals might have dictated the general view of ghosts.[81] There is an inconsistency here, in that if a person had been given the proper funeral and burial rituals, there was usually no need for him to return as a ghost. Winkler says that "a physical explanation sometimes given for the blackness of underworld ghosts is that cremation fires have charred the body and bones,"[82] but Russell may have a point in that the cremations had an influence on how the dead were perceived even outside of the underworld.

White ghosts, though less common in classical literature than in modern folklore, are perhaps more easily explained: their pure whiteness reflects the bloodless pallor of corpses.[83] It might even suggest the whiteness of skeletons; the word *larva,* which generally means "ghost," has also been used to mean "skeleton," as in Petronius (*Sat.* 34.8).[84] Examples of pale ghosts include Apuleius *Metamorphoses* 9.30, where a witch summons up the ghost of a woman who had been violently killed. The ghost is "ghastly pale" (*lurore buxeo*) and "horribly thin" (*macie foedata*).[85] At Petronius 62.10, the character Niceros, telling his werewolf story, says that after the shock of his frightening encounter with the creature, he arrived at his friend's house "pale as a ghost" (*ut larva intravi*). From the evidence, Winkler concludes, "While it is fairly common to find black robes mentioned as frightening, and to encounter a pallid spectre in a black robe, we have no examples of white-faced spectres in white robes," adding that, in contrast, "swathing oneself in a white sheet is the commonest impersonation of a ghost in American folklore." [86]

Although Winkler cites several examples of white-faced ghosts, he seems to have overlooked examples in both Greek and Latin literature of ghostly figures in white robes, including at least one clear instance in which the figures have white faces in addition to the white clothing. In Pliny the Younger 7.27.13, his slave-boy, describing a dream he had, says that "two men in white clothing" ("duo in tunicis albis") crept through the window and cut his hair as he was sleeping. Although it seems likely that the slave-boy is making up the story, Pliny himself suggests that the figures may be *phantasmata*. At least two incidents in Livy concern white-robed apparitions that were interpreted as portents. The first was in 218 B.C., when there came a report from Amiternum that figures of men dressed in white had been seen in several places but had not come near anyone (21.62.5–10). The second occurred in 214 B.C., at Hadria, when apparitions in white clothing were seen in the sky (24.10.10). Krauss suggests that the phantoms were probably thought of as spirits of the dead who formed a connecting link between the gods and men.[87] In Lucian's *Philopseudes* 25, Cleodemus tells a story of how he saw such an apparition when he was sick with fever: "There appeared at my side while I lay awake a very handsome young man, wearing a white cloak; then, raising me to my feet, he led me through a chasm to Hades." [88] Pausanias tells the story of how the Phocians were at war with the Thessalians. When the armies were lying opposite each other at the pass of Phocis, the Phocians attacked the Thessalians, first smearing their faces with chalk and donning white armor. The Thessalians thought this apparition of the night too unearthly to be an attack of their enemies, and, taking no action, were duly slaughtered by the Phocians (10.1.11). From these examples we can conclude that white-faced ghosts in white clothing were known in antiquity just as they are today.[89]

Perhaps more common than either black or white ghosts are ghosts that appear to be insubstantial and are only dimly visible. The descriptions of ghosts as smoke, clouds, dream-shapes, or shadows are familiar through-out Greek and Latin literature.[90] Plato, for example, describes "shadowy phantoms" (σκιοειδῆ φαντάσματα) flitting about graveyards and tombs (*Phd.* 81d). In Lucian's *Philopseudes* 16, a daimon that has been exorcised exits its host body like a puff of smoke. Ghosts in the underworld are no-toriously wraithlike, flitting about barely visible, as described in *Odyssey* 11. Actual cremations may have had an effect on this view of ghosts, too; whereas charred remains may have led to the perception of ghosts as black, the idea that the soul drifted off the pyre with the smoke may be responsible for the perception of ghosts as insubstantial and filmy.[91]

There are other descriptions of ghosts that Winkler does not discuss, because his aim is specifically to identify parallels to the masquerade of brigands in Lollianos's *Phoinikika*, where the villains paint themselves black and white. He does not include, for example, ghosts that are not described physically at all. Instances of this are rare, but we find an example in the *Mostellaria*, where the ghost's physical appearance is not described, and the storyteller arouses fear in his audience by other means. Several hauntings in antiquity are described mainly by sound rather than by sight, such as the haunted battlefield at Marathon (Paus. 1.32.4) and the haunted baths at Chaeronea (Plut. *Cim.* 1.6). Winkler also does not include examples of ghosts who appear as they looked in life, since these are regularly benign and fairly common.[92] Such is the case with the ghost of Patroclus that appears to Achilles at *Iliad* 23.64: he resembles his living form in size, clothing, voice, and look.[93] Even these lifelike ghosts turn out to be quite insubstantial, as Achilles finds out when he tries to embrace Patroclus.[94] The few representations of ghosts on Greek vase paintings depict figures that look no different from the living people often depicted on the same vases. One example is the red-figured vase on which Odysseus sees Elpenor coming out of the reeds in the marshy underworld.[95] Pausanias describes a painting depicting ghosts in the underworld, in which the Lesser Ajax, who had drowned, has the color of a drowned man with salt still on his skin; in the same painting, the dead Elpenor is simply dressed in a mat, such as sailors often wore (10.31).

Other ghosts that were not relevant to Winkler's discussion include ghosts that look as they did at the moment of their deaths, gory and wounded. The ghost of Sychaeus, appearing to Dido to say that her brother had murdered him, shows her the dagger wounds (Verg. *Aen.* 1.355). The image of Hector that appears to Aeneas in a dream at *Aeneid* 2.270ff. is particularly gruesome:

> There before my eyes, in a dream, appeared the desperately sad Hector, weeping many tears, torn by the chariot, as once before, and black with gory dust, walking on feet swollen by leather thongs . . . with a filthy beard and hair all stiff with blood, showing his wounds.[96]

Perhaps influenced by this passage about Hector, whose ghost tells Aeneas to flee the ruins of Troy, Ovid presents a similar situation in *Fasti* 3.639ff. The gory ghost of Dido, who killed herself when abandoned by Aeneas, appears to her sister Anna, who has taken refuge in the house of Aeneas and Lavinia. The ghost warns Anna to flee, because the jealous Lavinia is plotting against her: "It was night. Near her sister's bed seemed to stand Dido, covered in blood, with filthy hair, and she seemed to be saying 'Flee! Do not hesitate— Flee this dismal house!' " [97] Another example is that in Apuleius *Metamorphoses* 8.8, where the ghost of the murdered Tlepolemus, dripping with gore, appears to his wife in a dream to tell her who murdered him: "The ghost of Tlepolemus, miserably slaughtered, interrupted the chaste sleep of his wife, raising to her his face bloody with gore and hideously pale." [98]

These last few cases present ghosts that appeared to people in dreams. Winkler believes that the best approach to interpreting many of these ghostly phenomena is by way of Aristotle's analysis of dream-phantoms (*De somniis* 2–3). [99] Beginning with various types of misleading sense-impression, Aristotle focuses eventually on depressed states of awareness due to darkness or drowsiness. Minute visual impressions can seem, in the darkness, to be real shapes with lifelike movement.

Dreams, Ghosts, and Material Explanations

Though in general ghosts are thought of as somehow representing a person's soul, the materialization of immaterial beings presents a difficult problem. [100] Why, if the soul is spiritual, does the ghost appear in bodily shape? How can ghosts have the ability to speak? Questions such as these elicited the following sardonic comment from Ambrose Bierce, himself a renowned writer of ghost stories:

> There is one insuperable obstacle to a belief in ghosts. A ghost never comes naked; he appears either in a winding sheet or "in his habit as he lived." To believe in him, then, is to believe that not only have the dead the power to make themselves visible after there is nothing left of them, but that the same power inheres in textile fabrics. Supposing the products of the loom to have this ability, what object would they have in exercising it? and why does not the apparition of a suit of clothes sometimes walk abroad without a ghost in it? [101]

Though Bierce intended the comment humorously, he was not the first to raise this objection against a belief in ghosts. The question was a popular one, later addressed by Tyrrell:

> A characteristic of apparitions, which has given rise to some confusion, not to say ridicule, is that the central figure does not appear alone. It appears

with clothes on; and people have asked whether, in addition to believing in ghosts, they are expected to believe in ghostly skirts and ghostly trousers! The answer supplied by the evidence is quite definitive. They are not only expected to believe in ghostly skirts and trousers, but also in ghostly hats, sticks, dogs, horses, carriages, doors, curtains—anything, in fact, with which a human being is commonly surrounded. The difficulty in accepting these things is not really a difficulty at all. It arises from a false conception of what an apparition is.[102]

Tyrrell approaches the problem from a modern scientific standpoint, pointing out that one of the problems with many theories is that they consider apparitions to be physical entities. But where the physical theories are unpromising, he says, it is natural to try a psychological one instead.[103] Tyrrell suggests attempting to explain apparitions in terms of sensory perception, delving into the questions of telepathy and hallucination. One important observation Tyrrell draws from his case studies is that the majority of apparitions nowadays are seen by people who are on the verge of sleep— either just falling asleep or just waking up.[104] This suggests a connection between dreams and ghosts. Claire Russell emphasizes the importance of studying dreams and ghosts together, explaining that "a ghost may be a sort of veridical dream while awake . . . it must depend on a particular state of mind and mood to maintain that image."[105]

Many ghosts in classical literature appear to people in their dreams, and the Greeks and Romans clearly were not unaware of the connection. Lattimore, in his study of Greek and Roman epitaphs, concluded that the attitude toward dreams expressed in them indicated that dreams were seen as a bridge between the existent and the nonexistent.[106] The process of incubation, or temple-sleep, was long considered to be a way to contact the spirit world, because the mortal soul was thought to attain a higher state in dreams.[107] The interdependence of dreams and ghosts may also be reflected in the fact that in many of the earliest occurrences of ghosts in literature, the spirits appear in dreams, as, for example, Patroclus appears to Achilles. Also, dream-ghosts are almost invariably spirits of the newly deceased, for whom grief would be fresh, rather than of those who have been dead for many years.

The vocabulary used to describe many ghostly visits helps show the connection in antiquity between dreams and ghosts, even for ghosts that do not appear in dreams. The verbs ἐφίστημι (*ephistēmi*) and *adsisto,* which often describe figures in dreams, including ghosts, are also used frequently in descriptions of ghosts appearing to people who are awake. As Dodds observes,

"The dream is said not only to 'visit' the dreamer . . . but also to 'stand over' him (ἐπιστῆναι)." [108] For example, Pliny the Younger, in letter 3.5, applies *adstitit* to the ghost of Drusus Nero appearing to Pliny the Elder in a dream. Lucian uses forms of ἐφίστημι several times in his ghost stories, such as in the passage about Cleodemus's waking vision of the figure in white robes, given above (*Philops.* 25). Lucian also applies the verb twice to the ghost in his story about a haunted house at Corinth (ἐφίσταται, ἐπιστάς, *Philops.* 30–31). Phlegon describes the ghost of Polykritos as "the ghost standing nearby" (τὸν ἐπιστάντα δαίμονα) after it appears to a group of townspeople and waits impatiently nearby (*Mir.* 2).

From Aristotle on, many writers have commented on the connection between dreams and ghosts. Philosophers in antiquity even tried to make a scientific study of ghosts. The most elaborate approach was probably that of Democritus, who developed Leucippus's idea of atoms into a general theory of physics and physiology. His theory of vision was based on the idea that all objects give off thin films of atoms that drift around us and, when they impinge on the eyes or mind, create images. This theory explains virtually all supernatural phenomena. It explained ghosts, because the image-films could continue to drift around even after the sources (i.e., bodies) had decomposed.[109] Lucretius puts forth a similar atomic explanation of phantoms in his doctrine of *rerum simulacra* (1.127–35; 4.26–109; 724–822).[110] Aristotle, who does not actually discuss ghosts in any surviving passage, did think it possible to have a mixed state of sleeping and waking, as we have seen, and attributed dreams to the physical or mental state of the patient; he discusses precognitive dreams in several of his works, including *De divinatione per somnum* and *De somniis,* where he explains how sense-perception is affected when people are just dropping off to sleep or waking up (3.462a). Cicero expounds a theory of precognitive dreams in *De divinatione* and, unlike Aristotle, includes a few ghosts. We have already seen his story of the poet Simonides and the dead man who appeared in a dream to warn him of the shipwreck (1.27). Another story of a precognitive dream involving a ghost, which Cicero says is a well-known story, similarly reflects the desire for a proper burial:

> Once two friends from Arcadia were journeying together and came to Megara. There one of them lodged with an innkeeper, while the other went to stay with a host. They ate dinner and went to bed. At midnight the man staying with his host had a dream in which his friend at the inn appeared to him and begged for help, because the innkeeper was plotting his death. The man awoke, terrified at first by the dream; then he calmed

down and decided the dream did not mean anything, and went back to
sleep. But then in his dreams the same vision came again. This time it
asked him, since he had not helped his friend while he was alive, to at least
see that his death did not go unavenged. For his friend had been murdered
by the innkeeper and thrown into a wagon, and covered over with dung.
The vision beseeched the man to be at the town gate in the morning,
before the wagon could leave town. Then, much disturbed by the dream,
the man went in the morning to confront the driver at the gate, and asked
him what was in the wagon. Terrified, the driver fled, and the dead man
was found. When the affair came to light, the innkeeper was punished.[111]

This story, Cicero suggests, is proof of divine inspiration and shows that the
dead can communicate with the living.

But the prevailing view in antiquity seems to have been a rather skeptical one. Like Aristotle, most writers who had anything to say on the subject of apparitions suggested that they were dreams or hallucinations, with
no divine inspiration involved. This view is clearly stated in Plutarch *Brutus* 37.1–3, as the Epicurean Cassius tries to reassure Brutus that the baleful
apparition that appeared to him was not worth getting upset about: "We
do not really experience or see everything, but perception is a changeable
and tricky thing, and intelligence is very keen to change and transform the
thing from nothing to everything. . . . It is not believable that spirits exist,
or that if they do exist they have the shape or speech of men."[112] The Epicureans were the most resistant to the existence of supernatural phenomena
and tried to provide materialistic explanations for them; the Stoics and the
Pythagoreans, on the other hand, had little doubt as to the existence of
ghosts and prophetic visions. The Peripatos and the Academy took a more
ambiguous position.[113] In short, in antiquity there simply was no consensus concerning what ghosts consisted of and how they could make themselves seen. But the most popular theories suggested that the connection
between ghosts and the dream-state went a long way toward explaining the
phenomena.

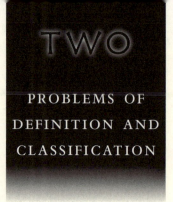

TWO

PROBLEMS OF
DEFINITION AND
CLASSIFICATION

IN ANTIQUITY, AS NOW, MANY DIFFERENT KINDS OF STORIES DEALT with supernatural topics, but in general the Greeks and Romans did not distinguish one supernatural event from another. Even today, classical scholars often consider stories of the supernatural as a homogeneous group. Wendland, for example, in his essay on ancient ghost stories, includes in his list the well-known werewolf story from Petronius's *Satyricon* 61–62.[1] Supernatural, yes—but not a *ghost* story. Knight makes the same generalization, including the werewolf story in his very brief discussion of ghosts. Admitting that he includes the story only because it is so interesting, he adds, "Werewolf phenomena are very strange. Perhaps they should be taken together and not compared with other kinds of occurrence."[2] What neither he nor Wendland states explicitly is that the spirits of the dead are not involved in werewolf stories, and consequently these tales cannot really be considered ghost stories.

As this problem demonstrates, clarification of the concept of "ghost" is needed on several points. There is, for one thing, a difference between our modern conception of the supernatural and the ancient one. Nowadays, ghost stories are concerned with "the intrusion of the mysterious, the supernatural within the context of everyday life; the clash between the rational and the irrational; the knowledge through direct revelation of a universe directed by forces beyond our comprehension."[3] But as Johnston points out, the term "supernatural" is very convenient for us because "it concisely subsumes a set of phenomena (ghosts, witches, vampires, incantations, potions, etc.) that, for contemporary Western readers, belong together."[4] She explains:

> It can be an acceptably convenient term to use when referring to ancient beliefs in such phenomena as well, if we first recognize that the ancient attitude towards them differed from the contemporary Western attitude in certain ways. To begin with, whereas most contemporary Americans and Europeans would see significant differences between the assumed natures

and activities of God and a ghost, the Greeks and Romans did not make any absolute *functional* distinction between the gods they worshipped in formal cult and the demonic beings whom they called upon in less formal settings. . . . To speak of the "supernatural" in opposition to the "natural" would have made little sense to people who understood all of these entities—humans, demons, and gods—to be functioning within the same physical space. They were all part of "nature" as the Greeks and Romans knew it.[5]

Since this was true of the ancient view of the world, some modern approaches to the supernatural in classical literature tend to deal with the subject in the same way, grouping all supernatural events together. We see this, for example, in Klotsche's article on the supernatural in the tragedies of Euripides: his study includes not only apparitions but prayers to the gods, curses, oaths, oracles, and prophecies. This is a rather overwhelming group of items to consider in the space of a journal article, and Klotsche has room to do little other than collect the material and state, "The difficulty still remains to reach tenable conclusions in regard to the poet's view of the supernatural."[6]

In the late nineteenth and early twentieth centuries, many scholars examining the supernatural in ancient literature tended, as Klotsche did, to group many disparate phenomena together and consider them from a religious point of view. The focus was often on the gods and how to communicate with them, and the category of "the supernatural" was too large to be dealt with effectively as a whole. It is possible, however, to consider hauntings as a distinct category of supernatural phenomena, and also to distinguish between certain types of ghostly manifestation. While there exists no standard view among folklorists, or even among parapsychologists, as to what a ghost is, we can define ghosts very broadly as the spirits of living beings who have died. How this spirit manifests itself is really the subject of our inquiry. The most common way a ghost manifests itself is as an apparition, an insubstantial or disembodied figure. But we may also speak of such a thing as an embodied ghost, or "revenant," and some types of ghostly phenomena, such as poltergeist activity, do not always involve the appearance of apparitions.

Terminology

The various words used for ghost in both Greek and Latin do not have very specific denotations. Besides φάσμα (*phasma*) and the variant φάντασμα (*phantasma*), Greek has several all-purpose words for apparition or ghost, including εἴδωλον (*eidōlon*) and δαίμων (*daimōn*). The latter often referred not just to ghosts but to evil spirits who might take possession of a person,[7] while *eidōlon* referred to apparitions of all sorts. Several other Greek words for "ghost" were used rather infrequently—σκιά (*skia*) meant a "shade" of the dead, and ψυχή (*psychē*) often referred not only to the soul but to the phantom of the deceased. In Homer, for example, "phantom" was one of the usual meanings of the word, and the image of Patroclus is referred to as *psychē* when it appears to Achilles in a dream (*Il.* 23.65).[8]

In Latin the terminology was equally vague. A late attempt to specify terms and classify different types of spirit was made by Apuleius in *De deo Socratis* 15: the *manes* are good spirits, not to be feared so long as their rites are duly performed; *lemures* are disembodied wandering spirits of the dead, thought of as mischievous and potentially dangerous to the living; and *larvae* are the ghosts that haunt houses. The phrase *larvis infestus* specifically applied to haunted houses; interestingly, we do not find this phrase in any of the surviving haunted-house stories. Apuleius is uncritical, the distinction between *larvae* and *lemures* is unclear,[9] and *manes* are not always benevolent. The term *manes* could be applied to angry ghosts thirsting for vengeance, as Livy uses it in 3.58.11 describing the ghost of Verginia (*manes Verginiae*), wandering from house to house seeking revenge.[10] *Larva*, interestingly, is one of the few words Pliny does *not* use to describe the ghost in his haunted-house story; he uses several others, however, including *idolon* (from the Greek), *umbra* ("shade," cf. Greek usage of σκιά), *monstrum, imago, simulacrum, effigies,* and finally *manes* (7.27.5–11). The many words were evidently interchangeable, and Vergil, for example, describes Creusa's ghost variously as *simulacrum, umbra,* and *imago* (*Aen.* 2.772–73, 793).[11] Various warning apparitions of giant women, discussed below, are not described in Latin with any of the usual words for "ghost," but rather are referred to as *species muliebris* or *mulieris,* whereas the Greek describes them with γυνή τις μείζων ἢ κατὰ ἀνθρώπου φύσιν ("a woman larger than normal human size") or other similar phrases.

In general, usages such as Pliny's and Vergil's were required simply for literary variation, and do not necessarily contain any more specific meanings than do the English synonyms "ghost," "phantom," "specter," "apparition," "shade," or "spook," the only difference being that some of the terms, such as "apparition," may be more general than others and can refer to types of visions other than those of disembodied, deceased beings. Luck observes that the English word "ghost" itself shows how ancient beliefs sometimes survive: it can mean "soul" or "spirit," as opposed to the body, but can also mean "a spectral apparition"; and in Christian belief, the Third Person of the Holy Trinity is called either the "Holy Spirit" or the "Holy Ghost." [12]

It is important to realize that ghosts are not one single phenomenon, but rather form a range of phenomena.[13] In antiquity, there were few real attempts at classification of ghosts; as we have seen, the terminology used to refer to types of ghost was vague, and the various words were often used synonymously. Using some of these vague distinctions that had been floating around for centuries, Tertullian divided the restless dead into three classes—those who had died before their time, the ἄωροι (aōroi) who had to wander till the span of their natural life was completed; those who had met with violent deaths, the βιαιοθάνατοι (biaiothanatoi); and the unburied, the ἄταφοι (ataphoi).[14] The categories are not mutually exclusive: there is nothing to prevent someone from being violently killed *and* left unburied. Also, these categories by no means cover the whole range of common ghostly phenomena described in antiquity. But if we examine the stories more carefully, we can see that several different categories of haunting emerge, each with particular characteristics.

Revenants

One category of supernatural story often identified as a ghost story involves reanimated corpses, usually called revenants or, more recently, "embodied ghosts."[15] One of the most well-known revenant stories from antiquity is that of Philinnion, found in the *Mirabilia* of Phlegon of Tralles, who was a freedman of the emperor Hadrian (A.D. 117–138).[16] The story, which is fragmentary, tells how a girl who was believed to be dead returned secretly to her parents' home and spent the nights with Machates, a male guest there. She had been reanimated by "divine will," and once her secret was discovered, she dropped dead again. Her body was indeed missing from the family vault and was lying instead in the family home. The townspeople burned the body outside of the city boundaries and performed apotropaic ceremonies. Meanwhile, when Machates realized what had happened, he killed himself (*Mir.* 1).[17]

The Greek vocabulary used in the story to describe the girl gives us a very good example of the lack of distinction between insubstantial apparitions and "embodied" ghosts. She is referred to several times as ἄνθρωπον (*anthrō-pon*, "person" or "human being") and several times by name (Φιλίννιον). When she drops dead, the corpse is variously referred to as νεκρά (*nekra*, "corpse") and σῶμα (*sōma*, "body"). At the very end of the story, however, perhaps for shock value, she is called φάσμα (*phasma*), a word usually translated as "apparition" or "phantom."[18] The term provides a jarring contrast to the otherwise corporeal words used to describe Philinnion.[19]

Lawson, drawing a distinction between revenant stories and ghost stories, observes:

> Most emphatically this is no ghost-story. The distinction between ghosts and Greek *revenants* is of a primary and universal nature, patent to all who can discriminate between soul and body. In this story Philinnion acts as a *revenant* and is treated as a *revenant;* the inspection of the vault in which her body had been laid and the purpose of her nocturnal visits to Machates furnish conclusive evidence of her corporeal resuscitation.[20]

Lawson does not address the problem of terminology. He does, however, argue against modern classification of revenant tales as ghost stories, and explains that the ancient Greeks did draw a distinction between reanimated corpses (body) and ghosts (soul).[21] Stories of revenants have characteristics different from those of stories of unsubstantial apparitions, just as tales of "warning apparitions" have characteristics peculiar to themselves, as discussed below. Philinnion, and other revenants, do not come back for the same reasons other ghosts return. Philinnion was not improperly buried, and her spirit was not restless.[22] Technically, such stories are of reanimated corpses, which are rather different from ghosts, but the ancient Greeks had no separate term to describe revenants. Phlegon himself, having applied the word *phasma* to the corporeal Philinnion, also uses it in several other stories to describe insubstantial apparitions. He follows the story of Philinnion with the story of Polykritos, who returns from the dead by suddenly appearing at a town meeting and requesting that his child, a hermaphrodite, be handed over to him. When the townspeople hesitate, the ghost (*phasma*) seizes the child, tears it limb from limb, and devours all of it but the head. The people throw stones at the ghost, which is physically unaffected, and after its ghoulish feast, the ghost simply disappears (*Mir.* 2).

Similar to the revenants described by Phlegon is the ghost that appears in Pausanias's story of the Hero of Temesa (6.6.7–11), also found in Strabo 6.1.5. As Pausanias tells it, Odysseus and his crew were once forced ashore at Temesa by a storm. There one of his sailors got drunk and raped a local girl, and the people of Temesa stoned him to death. Odysseus apparently did not care, and simply sailed away. But the ghost (*daimōn*) of the stoned man began killing the inhabitants of Temesa until they consulted the Pythia, who told them to propitiate the ghost by dedicating a sanctuary to him and giving him every year the most beautiful maiden in the town. One day the famous boxer Euthymus came to Temesa just at the time the people were propitiating the ghost. Euthymus fell in love with the girl, who swore to marry him if he saved her. So Euthymus waited for the daimon and won a fight with him, driving the ghost out of the land. The ghost disappeared, sinking into the sea, and Euthymus married the girl.

The "ghost" must have had a substantial body, as functional as any person's and even stronger in order to cause such destruction and wrestle with Euthymus.[23] The story of the Hero of Temesa has many traditional elements familiar from folktales and heroic literature. Euthymus's waiting up for the ghost is reminiscent of Grettir waiting up for the ghost of Glam in the Icelandic *Grettir's Saga*, or Beowulf waiting for Grendel in the Anglo-Saxon epic *Beowulf*. Like Glam, the Greek ghost was physically dangerous; like Grendel, he was driven into the water. The rescue of the girl is related to the folktale type in which girls are saved from monsters, such as in the legend of Perseus. Such tales may be relics of human sacrifice, and in the case of the ghost of Temesa, we may have an instance of human sacrifice at the tomb of a dead warrior, such as the legendary sacrifices at the tombs of Patroclus and Achilles.[24]

The Hero of Temesa is not the only hero whose ghost ought to be classified as a revenant. Dead heroes in general, unlike other dead people, apparently constituted a special class as far as the Greeks and Romans were concerned. The spirits of heroes were confined within the boundaries of their native countries, the neighborhoods of their graves, or the sites of their cults.[25] Many are described in the ancient writers as having the ability to interact physically with the living. Sometimes this interaction comes about because the hero has been angered, as in the cases of the Hero of Temesa and the hero Eunostos at Tanagra. The latter was killed through the treachery of a woman, and would tolerate no woman near his grave. If any woman came near, the spirit of Eunostos would cause an earthquake or drought.[26] Pausanias records a story circulated by the people of Orchomenos about a similarly destructive hero-ghost. A ghost was ravaging the land. The people asked the Delphic Oracle what to do about this, and the god told them to find the remains of the hero Actaeon and bury them. He also told them to make a bronze statue of the ghost and fasten it to a rock with iron. They did so, and the destruction ceased. Pausanias reports that he himself had seen this statue (9.38.5).

More often, the ghosts of heroes manifested themselves physically by fighting in battle and killing many of the enemy soldiers. Plutarch in his *Life of Theseus* (35.5) says that "Many of the Greeks who fought the Persians at Marathon thought they saw an apparition of Theseus in armor fighting on their side against the barbarians."²⁷ Pausanias, describing the part of the Painted Stoa at Athens with a scene of the battle at Marathon, notes that in addition to the hero Marathon, there was a depiction of Theseus rising from the underworld to fight in the battle (1.15.3). When the Persians came back, under the command of Xerxes, miraculous sightings of heroes fighting on the side of the Greeks continued: Herodotus reports that the Delphians were aided in their fight by "two hoplites of larger than human stature who pursued the Persians and cut them down."²⁸ The phantom fighters were later said to be the native heroes Phylacus and Autonous (8.38–39).²⁹

Herodotus also tells the unusual story of the ghost of a hero who returned not to fight, but to procreate. The mother of Demaratus of Sparta claimed to have conceived him not with his father Ariston, but with a phantom who looked like Ariston. The phantom put a wreath it was wearing on her head, then went away. When Ariston returned and asked where she got the wreath, she said that Ariston himself had given it to her. The confusion was cleared up when the wreath was discovered to be from the shrine of the hero Astrabacus, and the woman was told that it was the phantom of Astrabacus who must have visited her (6.69).³⁰ In his alleged physical desire, this hero more resembles Philinnion than the ghosts of other heroes.

In many of these cases, labeling the heroes as "revenants" is problematic. Although they can affect people physically—they can kill or procreate—they generally vanish suddenly without leaving their bodies behind, unlike Phlegon's Philinnion, or Apuleius's Socrates in *Metamorphoses* 1.13– 19. Socrates has been brutally murdered by two witches, who then reanimate his corpse by stanching the wound with a sponge and casting a spell on it. To the amazement of his companion, Socrates wakes up in the morning without a trace of his horrible wound. But when he tries to cross a stream, the spell is broken and he drops dead.³¹ Apuleius never applies any of the Latin words for ghost to Socrates, nor does he invent a Latin term for "revenant"; instead, he describes Socrates as a *corpus exanimatum* ("lifeless body"), and that only when the unfortunate Socrates dies for the second time.

There are other, briefer reports of such reanimated corpses. Pliny the Elder, for example, says that Varro records a story of a person who was being carried out for burial but returned home on foot (*HN* 7.52). Pliny also tells how one man came to life again on the funeral pyre, but the flames were already too hot and no one could rescue him, so he died again (*HN* 7.52). Plato, introducing his myth of Er, tells how Er was killed in battle, was lying on the funeral pyre, came to life again, and reported what he had seen in the other world (*Rep.* 10.614b). Phlegon includes a short story about a soldier named Bouplagos who had fallen in battle from twelve wounds, but suddenly at midday stood up and uttered prophecies before expiring again. Badly shaken, the generals decided to give Bouplagos priority and quickly cremated him (*Mir.* 3).

Crisis Apparitions and Other Portentous Phantoms

Another type of supernatural manifestation is the crisis apparition. Crisis apparitions are phantoms of friends or relatives that appear just as they undergo some great trauma, injury, or death—for example, the apparition of a soldier appearing to his mother at the moment he is killed in battle. These apparitions appear only once, at the moment of crisis, but are generally considered to "haunt" even though they do not recur.[32] Sometimes they are referred to as "ghosts of the dying."[33]

The cases of crisis apparitions reported in antiquity are few,[34] but they include the story of one of the most famous ghosts from classical literature, the ghost of Creusa, wife of Aeneas. Leading his family from the burning city of Troy, Aeneas looks back and realizes that Creusa is no longer with the group (Verg. *Aen.* 2.723ff.). Greatly distressed, he returns to Troy to search for her, finding his house in flames and Priam's palace plundered. As Aeneas frantically wanders the streets, he is met by Creusa's ghost. Vergil never explicitly states that Creusa has died, but he refers to her with several of the more common Latin words for ghost, including *simulacrum, imago,* and *umbra:* "An unhappy phantom, the ghost of Creusa herself, appeared before my eyes, an apparition larger than life" (*infelix simulacrum atque ipsius umbra Creusae / visa mihi ante oculos et nota maior imago,* 2.772–73). Although in general Latin usage both *simulacrum* and *imago* may refer to apparitions that are not necessarily ghosts of dead people, Vergil himself often uses both *imago* and *umbra* to refer specifically to ghosts (cf. *Aen.* 1.353, 4.386, 6.480 and 695). Creusa's own explanation of her fate is rather mysterious: she says, "The Great Mother of the gods detains me on these shores" (*me magna deum genetrix his detinet oris,* 2.788), and she is not among the ghosts Aeneas meets in the underworld. It is clear, however, that Creusa as Aeneas knew her had died, and this apparition appears either at the very moment of her death or just after it. The ghost tells Aeneas not to indulge in grief, but to go on without her, and prophesies his future: after much wandering, he will have joy, a kingdom, and a new wife.[35] And so the "crisis" of this particular apparition is twofold: this is not only the moment of Creusa's passing, but also the moment when Aeneas realizes he has a duty beyond that of his immediate family and the doomed city of Troy.

A similar story is told of Romulus, the founder of Rome. After his death, Romulus appeared to Julius Proculus to say that he was now a god named Quirinus and a shrine should be built for him on the Quirinal hill. Ovid describes the apparition of Romulus as "noble, and larger than human" (*pulcher et humano maior, Fasti* 2.503). This is a good example of a crisis apparition: the phantom is that of a known person appearing recently after his death, to explain his fate. Like Creusa, this phantom helps to resolve a difficulty, because the Romans were despondent at the loss of their leader and took heart when Proculus reported the incident to them. Livy's version of the story is more cynical, suggesting that it was a shrewd political move by Proculus to invent such a story (1.16.5–8).

Another example of a crisis apparition occurs in Apuleius *Metamorphoses* 9.31. The ghost of a father appears to his daughter, who lives in a nearby village, to tell her how he has just been killed: "During the night her father's mournful phantom appeared to her, with a noose around his neck, and told her the whole story about the crime of her stepmother . . . and how through her spells he had descended to the underworld."[36] The next day her father's body is discovered hanging from a roofbeam. The phrase "during the night" (*per quietem*) implies that the apparition appeared in the middle of the night and so possibly in the daughter's dream, but Apuleius does not specifically say this. If the phantom appeared to the daughter while she was awake, it is a particularly good example of a crisis apparition. If it appeared in her dream, it is more closely related to Cicero's discussion about prophetic dreams and his story about the traveling friends from Arcadia (*Div.* 1.27, discussed in Chapter 1).

Related to crisis apparitions are so-called warning apparitions,[37] phantoms appearing in order to utter a prophecy or warning to the percipient. These differ slightly from crisis apparitions in that they are not phantom forms of friends or relatives appearing at times of personal crisis, though both types of apparition are prophetic in nature. Warning apparitions cannot even be clearly identified as ghosts, because they are not the spirits of people who have died. They seem, instead, to be semi-deities or divine messengers of some sort, halfway between gods and ghosts. But this particular type of apparition occurs so frequently in classical literature that any discussion of ghost stories in antiquity would be negligent in omitting it.

Several characteristics common to most warning apparitions described in classical literature help identify such phantoms as a distinct group: the apparitions appear as waking visions rather than in dreams; they are described as being of unusually large stature; and they warn or prophesy by direct speech or figurative action. Also, most of these phantoms are female; they appear during wartime, military campaign, or other politically critical situations; and a portent in nature, such as an earthquake, may accompany their appearance. Nearly all the stories of warning apparitions occur in the writings of historians.

One example of this type of portentous phantom is the apparition of a woman who appears to Curtius Rufus and foretells his governorship of Africa. The story is related by Pliny the Younger as well as Tacitus. Pliny, who gives us a more detailed version than that of Tacitus, describes the incident as follows (7.27.2−3):

> At that time [Curtius Rufus] was unimportant and unknown, and went as an attendant to the new governor of Africa. One afternoon he was walking in the portico. There appeared to him the figure of a woman, larger than human and more beautiful. He was terrified, but she said to him that she was Africa and had come to tell his future: that he would go to Rome where he would hold office and then return to that province with highest honor and die there. Everything that she said came true. Moreover, it is said that the same figure appeared to him on the shore as he arrived in Carthage and was disembarking from the ship. What is certain is that when he fell ill, he despaired and held no hope of recovering his health, though none of his friends were despairing; he expected the future part of her prediction to come true based on the past events, and predicted that misfortune based on his success.[38]

Pliny describes the apparition as "a figure larger than human and more beautiful" (*figura humana grandior pulchriorque*), and Tacitus describes her as "a type of woman beyond human measure" (*species muliebris ultra modum humanum, Ann.* 11.21). Creusa's ghost, too, is described as larger than human (*nota maior imago, Aen.* 2.773), which may hint at apotheosis, in keeping with Creusa's mysterious fate.[39] Other reports of female warning figures contain similar descriptions. Suetonius reports that Drusus ceased his pursuit of the enemy into Germany when the apparition of a giant barbarian woman, who conveniently happened to speak Latin, warned him not to press any farther: "A kind of barbarian woman larger than human forbade them, in Latin, to continue their successful attack any farther" (*species barbarae mulieris humana amplior victorem tendere ultra sermone Latino prohibuisset, Claud.* 1). Dio Cassius records a similar incident (55.1.3), saying that Drusus failed in his attempt to cross the Elbe when a gigantic woman appeared and said that it was not his fate to go any farther, and that he was soon to die:

"A woman of much larger size than normal stood by him and said, 'Where do you think you're going, insatiable Drusus? You are not fated to go farther. Stop here; for the end of both your journey and your life is at hand.'" [40] Herodotus reports a story that was circulating about how, during the battle at Salamis, "the phantom of a woman appeared and urged them on loudly, so that the entire Greek army could hear, first berating them thus: 'You wretches! How much farther do you intend to retreat?'" (Hdt. 8.84.2). [41]

Plutarch records that both Dion and Brutus were warned of their imminent deaths by the appearance to each of an ominous apparition (*Dion* 2.1–2). Dion was sitting alone late one day, when "a phantom appeared to Dion, huge and portentous. . . . He saw a large woman passing by, in dress and countenance like a tragic Fury." [42] Brutus, sitting alone in quiet thought late at night, "saw a strange and terrible apparition, of unnatural and fearful form" (ὁρᾷ δεινὴν καὶ ἀλλόκοτον ὄψιν ἐκφύλου σώματος καὶ φοβεροῦ). When he addressed it, the figure replied, "I am your own evil spirit, Brutus; you shall see me at Philippi" (ὁ σός, ὦ Βροῦτε, δαίμων κακός· ὄψει δέ με περὶ Φιλίππους, *Brut.* 36.3–4). [43]

In the case of Brutus, the figure that appeared was evidently male. Male warning apparitions appear less frequently in the extant literature than female warning figures do, and they are more reticent than the females. One such apparition appeared to Julius Caesar as he hesitated before crossing the Rubicon. According to Suetonius (*Iul.* 32),

A man of extraordinary size and form suddenly appeared, sitting nearby playing a reed pipe; a group of shepherds gathered to listen, and even some of the soldiers from the camp, including some of the trumpeters, ran up to hear. At this he ran down to the river, having snatched a trumpet from one of them, and blowing a great blast on the trumpet, he crossed over to the other bank. [44]

Though this figure did not speak, his actions were clearly significant, indicating that Caesar's campaign would be successful.

As we have seen above, larger-than-normal figures, often those of heroes, appear during times of battle and, since they are able to affect people physically, might be considered revenants. In addition to the two Delphian heroes who appeared during the battle of Marathon, Herodotus (6.117.3) reports the story told by Epizelus, an Athenian soldier who fought in the battle: suddenly during the battle he lost his vision, though nothing had touched him, and he remained blind for the rest of his life. He said that "a large armed man stood opposite him, whose beard overshadowed his shield—but the apparition passed by him and instead killed the man standing next to him."[45] Another example, from Dio Cassius, tells how Trajan was saved from the earthquake at Antioch (A.D. 115) by a superhuman figure: "Trajan escaped from the building he was in when there came to him a figure larger than human, who led him outside, so that he survived unharmed."[46] In this case, the figure interacts physically with the percipient.

Lucian, describing a similar type of apparition, this time another female phantom, exaggerates her size even more: "I saw a fearful woman coming toward me, nearly half a stadion tall" (γυναῖκα ὁρῶ προσιοῦσαν φοβεράν, ἡμισταδιαίαν σχεδὸν τὸ ὕψος, *Philops.* 20). The apparition turns out to be the goddess Hekate, but Lucian is clearly following the "warning apparition" prototype: his version is notable as a satire of precisely the category of phantom under discussion and the circumstances under which such a phantom appears. The giant Hekate, bearing a torch and a sword, does not appear during a battle or any other critical situation, though she materializes as Eucrates is walking alone in the woods at midday, one of the times for supernatural occurrences. He hears dogs barking, followed directly by an earthquake and thunder. Hekate appears, accompanied by dogs "larger than Indian elephants," and opens up a rift in the earth through which Eucrates can view Hades. Hekate leaps into the chasm, while Eucrates sees his own father among the dead, "wearing the same clothes he had on when we buried him" (*Philops.* 22–23).

One of the main differences between crisis apparitions and warning apparitions is that the former are spirits of the dead, while the latter are less personal, semi-divine entities. What distinguishes these types of otherworldly visitation, however, is that they are usually triggered not by the circumstances of a person's death, but by the need of the percipient. Although the apparition of the murdered father in Apuleius *Metamorphoses* 9.31 visits his daughter to tell her of his murder, the phantoms of Creusa, Romulus, and most of the warning apparitions listed here appear not in order to focus on themselves, but to focus on the percipient.[47] The emotional states of the percipients play a large role in these incidents. Creusa appears to Aeneas when he is frantically searching for her, at the risk of his own life; warning apparitions are recorded at the onset of difficult military ventures, such as the battle of Salamis and the crossing of the Rubicon, when the percipients are under stress. Dion and Brutus privately see apparitions on the eve of battle, when they are in states of heightened anxiety.[48]

Reports of such apparitions must also have acted as a kind of political propaganda. The appearance of these phantoms in times of crisis was used to justify subsequent actions and events. They indicated that outcomes such as victory or defeat in battle, or an individual's survival or death, were divinely sanctioned. Many of these apparitions appeared to important political figures, such as Aeneas, Julius Proculus, Julius Caesar, Brutus, and Trajan. Hopkins, discussing how Romans like Pliny (the Younger) had an affinity for ghost stories, has remarked that "modern historians of Rome usually underrate the importance of beliefs in the supernatural in Roman politics."[49] The characteristics of these phantoms, and their frequent appearance in classical literature, in fact speak for their importance. Although there is no telling whether the historians who recorded these stories actually believed them, the stories were nevertheless circulating in society and were meant to impress upon people the idea that important political successes such as the Athenian victory at Salamis or Caesar's crossing the Rubicon had a touch of divine approval about them. Similarly, the defeats and deaths of important figures, accompanied by such portentous phantoms, would also have been seen as destined by fate.

Poltergeists

Another ghostly phenomenon is the "poltergeist," from the German word meaning "noisy ghost"—so called because poltergeists cause a great deal of noise. Typical of poltergeist activity are crashing sounds or rappings on walls and doors. Poltergeists can also be very physical, as their manifestations may include furniture moving across the room or crockery flying off the shelves. Poltergeist activity tends to be short-lived, lasting from a few days to a couple of months. It is an especially interesting type of haunting: poltergeist manifestations usually center on a particular person, rather than a particular place. That is, though many ghosts are bound to specific locations and can be seen by anybody who happens to be there, poltergeists move around with a particular person as their focus and are usually experienced only by that person and others who happen to be nearby.[50] It is often an adolescent who serves as the focus for poltergeist activity, a young person who not only attracts the phenomena but is thought somehow to cause them by telepathic means. When this young person leaves the house, the phenomena cease, but may recur in the new location; therefore, the house itself is not considered to be haunted, though the person is.

Although poltergeists are regularly reported from medieval times onward, there are few incidents reported in antiquity that describe poltergeist activity, and there was no word or concept in antiquity corresponding to our usage of "poltergeist." This is largely because what we consider poltergeist manifestations would have been considered portents in antiquity. A rain of stones, for example, which is nowadays often associated with poltergeist activity, was a frequent type of portent in Livy.[51] And so Dodds reports, "I have never come across a recognizable pre-Christian tale of a poltergeist," though he goes on to describe several stories from antiquity that *might* have qualified as poltergeist phenomena if only they had been reported as recurrent rather than isolated incidents. He cites, for instance, this tale from Suetonius (*Aug.* 6):[52]

> In a villa in an ancestral suburb near Velitra, a very small room, like a pauper's garret, is shown as the place where Augustus was brought up, and the consensus around the neighborhood is that he was also born there. Because of an old rumor, no one dares enter the room unless it is necessary, and after purification. It is as if a certain horror and dread prevent those approaching casually from entering. The reason for this dread was recently made plain: for when the new owner of the villa, whether by chance or to tempt fate, decided to sleep in the bed in that room one night, it happened that after a few hours he was thrown out of the bed by a sudden unknown force and was found semiconscious in front of the doors along with the bedclothes.[53]

Dodds notes another case, Andocides 1.30, that sounds more like regular poltergeist activity:

> "Hipponicus keeps an evil spirit (*aliterion*) in his house, who upsets his table (*trapeza*)." Nothing supernormal is intended here: the "evil spirit" in question is Hipponicus' spendthrift son, and the word *trapeza* is introduced for the sake of a pun on its secondary meaning "bank" (Hipponicus was a wealthy financier). But the joke would have additional point if the speaker's audience were familiar with stories of real poltergeists.[54]

One story from Lucian may qualify as a poltergeist incident: In *Philopseudes* 21, the physician Antigonus tells about his little bronze figurine of the great doctor Hippocrates. "As soon as the light is out," he says, "the figurine goes all around the house making noises, overturning the vials, mixing up the medicines and knocking over the mortar, especially when we've postponed our annual sacrifice to him."[55] I tend to agree with Dodds, however, who says of this episode, "The walking statue which upset the doctor's pharmacy . . . looks like an instance [of poltergeist activity]; but the parody is aimed at the belief in animated images rather than poltergeists."[56]

Continual Apparitions

Continual apparitions constitute the most widespread type of apparition reported in ghost-lore. Usually described as recurring repeatedly over a period of time, they are the kind of ghost most frequently associated with hauntings. There are two main types of continual apparition.

Some continual apparitions, frequently called "recordings," are connected to past events that are somehow "recorded" at the location where they happened and then "replayed" at certain other times.[57] Many ghosts of historical figures fall into this category, and particular buildings, such as Hampton Court in England, are reputedly haunted by several famous ghosts. One rumor, for example, concerns Catherine Howard, who tried to escape her captors and appeal to her husband Henry VIII by running down a corridor toward the chapel he was in: her ghost is reputedly seen running down that same corridor periodically.[58] A variant rumor reports that her screams of terror are still heard in the Haunted Chamber.[59] Similarly, the Tower of London is considered one of the most haunted places in England because of the many people who met miserable deaths there, and there have often been reports of the ghost of Anne Boleyn being seen around the Tower, both with her head and without it.

One of the most popular types of recording is the ghostly army engaging in battle over and over again. We have an example of this from antiquity in Pausanias's report that often on the plain of Marathon, at night, the neighing of horses and sounds of men fighting can be heard, as if the battle were still being fought (1.32.4).[60] Reports of ghostly armies were frequent in antiquity, and many were single-occurrence sightings rather than continually haunted locations. We have already seen several stories from Herodotus concerning phantom figures appearing during battles such as Marathon. Many single-occurrence sightings of ghostly armies were interpreted as prodigies, such as the one described by Pliny the Elder, who says that during the wars in northern Germany, a clashing of arms and the sound of a trumpet were heard from the sky (*HN* 2.58). Pliny also reports that during the third consulship of Marius, the inhabitants of Ameria and Tuder saw armies in the sky advancing from the east and west to meet in battle, with those from the west being defeated (*HN* 2.58).[61] Similar celestial armies were seen during Titus's attack on Jerusalem, as reported by Tacitus (*Hist.* 5.13). In Lucan's *Pharsalia,* portents of war include the noise of unseen armies coming to blows: "Urns filled with the bones of dead men gave forth groans. Then the clashing of weapons and loud cries were heard in the pathless groves, and ghosts coming together in combat" (1.568–70).[62] Shortly after this, the ghost of Sulla rose up from the Campus Martius and uttered prophecies, while the ghost of Marius broke out of its tomb and raised its head toward the Anio River, sending the farmers fleeing in fear (1.580–83).

Another example of a recording-type haunting from antiquity may be found in Plutarch's account of how, in his native city of Chaeronea, a bandit named Damon had been murdered in the baths, and ghosts continued to haunt the spot afterward (*Cim.* 1.6): "For a long time certain apparitions appeared at the place, and groans were heard, as our ancestors tell us, and the doors of the bath were walled up."[63]

Aside from "recordings," the main type of continual apparition in classical literature is the "interactive" ghost. This type of ghost appears to be aware of a person's presence: it may respond to words and gestures, may gesture back and attempt to speak, and may follow the percipient.[64] In modern times, it is the interactive type of ghost that is considered the principal evidence for the survival of the spirit after death, and it may have been so in antiquity as well. Interactive ghosts intentionally seek communication with the living. They come to warn or advise, or to ask for help, or to take revenge. In cases of "recordings," there is usually no attempt to lay the ghost to rest and clear the haunted spot. Pausanias does not say that anyone ever tried to purify the Marathon battlefield, and Plutarch says that the hauntings at the Chaeronea bath continued into his own time, with no indication that rituals were ever performed to drive away the disturbing ghosts. No one tries to exorcise Hampton Court or the Tower of London. (That might drive tourists away.) Interactive continual apparitions, however, are usually taken care of. They either indicate somehow to the living that they wish the proper rituals to be performed or some other unfinished task to be completed, or they make such a nuisance of themselves that people are compelled to take action against them. It is interactive ghosts that are most frequently associated with haunted houses, the subject of the next chapter.

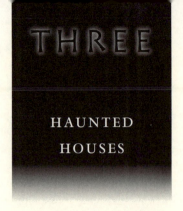

THREE

HAUNTED HOUSES

STORIES OF HAUNTED HOUSES, ANCIENT AND MODERN, ORAL AND literary, tend to have certain elements in common besides the haunting itself.[1] There are "symptoms" characteristic of a haunted house, such as the physical condition of the house and the types of paranormal phenomena reported to have occurred there. Many tales of haunted houses, including the extant stories from antiquity, share a common narrative pattern as well, a plot that culminates in a showdown between the ghost and the story's protagonist. One particularly interesting feature of such stories is their inclusion of realistic details, for example, specific information regarding the difficulty in selling or renting out a haunted property. Accounts of haunted houses from Greece and Rome suggest that disclosure laws concerning haunted property have not changed much in two thousand years.

Symptoms

Modern haunted-house stories, particularly those circulated orally, often begin with a description of the physical setting, including the size and condition of the house itself. The story may open with a stock phrase, such as "There is an old mansion," or "There is a big estate," and the large house is deserted or dilapidated.[2] Grider has observed that contemporary ghost stories about haunted houses generally dismiss the exterior of the house with such simple openings because no further description is necessary: the image of a haunted house is already well fixed through literature and popular culture. The action of a good ghost story should take place *inside* the haunted house.[3] We do not have enough descriptions of haunted buildings from antiquity to know whether a fixed image for haunted sites also existed then. Sherwin-White, searching for an explanation as to why we have relatively few such stories from antiquity, suggests that the dearth "may be due in part to the material factor of the classical environment. The relatively small size, and the compact building, of houses even of the wealthy classes, and the preponderance of urban life, did not allow the free development of the 'haunted house' and 'lonely castle' themes dear to the ghostly literature of the nineteenth century."[4] It is true that large houses were relatively rare, and the few haunted-house stories from antiquity do show some awareness of the need for a certain type of large, eerie setting. Pliny the Younger opens his narrative by specifying that the house was "large and roomy," and he stresses the fact that the house was deserted (7.27.5–11). In Lucian, the haunted house has been abandoned, and its roof is falling in (*Philops.* 30). Plutarch, describing the haunted baths at Chaeronea (*Cim.* 1.6), says that they were abandoned and boarded up. Clearly, this stock detail has very early origins. As Luck points out, "People shunned haunted places then as now because they often indicated the presence of evil—murder, for instance, or [other] violent death."[5]

Haunted houses are generally characterized by continual apparitions, less often by poltergeist activity. The apparitions recur frequently over time and are witnessed by many different people. Many mysterious and inexplicable phenomena have been attributed to haunted sites over the centuries. Nardi catalogues a number of them, noting that they appeal to various senses—hearing, vision, smell, and touch.[6] The manifestations fall into several categories. The first category includes sounds of all kinds that have no apparent cause, including, for example, furniture falling over, glass breaking, doors and windows closing violently, weights being dragged across the floor, human footsteps, the rustle of clothing, and cries, groans, sobs, sighs, and singing. Usually no physical evidence for these manifestations is found.

The second category includes events that do produce physical evidence in addition to sounds; for example, furniture moves across the room, doors and windows *are* slammed shut, crockery is broken, bells are rung by unseen hands. Other, more rare occurrences in this category include a person's being thrown out of bed, the mysterious disappearance and reappearance of various household objects, spontaneous fires in the house, and even a rain of stones. This category includes many phenomena usually attributed to poltergeists, and we have seen, for example, the case from Suetonius in which a man staying in Augustus's boyhood home was mysteriously tossed to the floor (*Aug.* 6).

The last category of phenomena is most closely associated with the continual apparitions of haunted houses. This category includes visual rather than auditory phenomena, mainly apparitions of human beings known to be deceased. Often they are clothed as in life; sometimes they appear to be solid, at other times transparent. They may be seen passing through walls or doors, walking or gliding through the air. Such apparitions appear intermittently, for a fixed and usually brief period of time, and they may be preceded by the sensation of a "presence" in the room. The proximity of such an apparition is sometimes accompanied by a chill breeze. Sometimes the apparition moves like a sleepwalker and remains unaware of any people present (a "recording"), or it may respond to gestures and words, and even try to communicate (an "interactive" apparition).[7] More rarely, the apparition is that of an animal rather than a human. The percipient may sense a weight or pressure on part of his or her body, or even the contact of icy hands; and there may be an odd smell in the air, such as an unfamiliar perfume or, rarely, a more unpleasant, even cadaverous stench.

The hauntings recorded in classical literature generally do not include extensive lists of phenomena such as the ones given here for haunted sites in general. Most frequently the classical hauntings involve an apparition, sometimes accompanied by sounds, such as groans or the rattling of chains, as for example in the haunted baths at Chaeronea (Plut. *Cim.* 1.6) or the house at Athens described by Pliny the Younger (7.27.5–11). Other hauntings in antiquity involved only sound, such as in Pausanias's description of the neighing of horses and clashing of arms heard at the site of the battle of Marathon (1.32.4). Aside from the revenants discussed in Chapter 2, it is unusual to find a haunting described by touch, and none of the ghost stories from antiquity mention any odd or unfamiliar smells accompanying a haunting.

A Popular Plot

The most complete haunted-house stories from antiquity are those of Plautus, Pliny, and Lucian. With only three stories extant, we cannot state definitively that all haunted-house stories had the same basic plot. There may have been many variations that simply do not survive. Yet the three surviving stories share very similar plot lines, and we can hypothesize that the authors who recorded these stories may have been working from a commonly known narrative structure, or at least a particularly popular one.

In folklore as well as in literature, it is possible to trace patterns of narrative and "assess the interaction of religious information and fictional imagination."[8] Winkler has identified three kinds of connection among various instances of the same narrative pattern. First, there is sometimes a direct literary dependence, where an author read and drew on his predecessors. It is often difficult, however, to prove this dependence, though *imitatio* and *variatio* can strongly suggest the literary connection. Second, different versions of a narrative may come from a tradition of oral folk-narrative, which can explain certain specificity of detail. Third, at some level of fundamental experience, it makes sense to say that two stories are alike because the basic elements of the situation described from real life are alike. That is, there can be a narrative interdependence through common social experience; individual details may be different, of course, because we would expect that an author using a narrative formula would try to vary the details.[9] It is possible for us to establish a common narrative structure for the three major extant haunted-house stories, and since there is no evidence of direct dependence of one on another, the second of Winkler's three connections clearly applies here.

Radermacher's study of Lucian's *Philopseudes* summarizes the plot common to the three haunted-house stories surviving from antiquity. In comparing the ghost stories found in Lucian, Pliny, and Plautus, Radermacher finds the following basic narrative structure. At some time before the setting of the story, a guest has been killed and buried on the grounds. Since the murder, the spirit of the deceased walks at night, until a courageous man comes along, who resolves to find the cause of the haunting. He follows the ghost and marks the spot where the remains are presumably buried, and, after a proper burial of the bones, tranquility returns to the house.[10] Radermacher's discussion, brief though it is, is still considered the standard work on ancient haunted houses. Nardi considers Radermacher the main authority at least on these three authors' ghost stories, noting that he most clearly explicates the unity of the story archetype.[11]

Yet Radermacher clearly makes several assumptions for which there is no basis in the stories. For example, he refers to the ghost as that of a "Gast" and an "Ermordeten," a houseguest who was subsequently a murder victim,[12] which is definitely the case in Plautus's story but is not stated in Pliny's or Lucian's. This particular point, however, is not essential to the story archetype.[13] Radermacher is basically trying to get at the idea that an improper burial is often the underlying cause for the ghost's wanderings, and one of the most frequent reasons for lack of burial in antiquity is indeed this gross violation of the guest-host relationship. Examples of this include the case of Polydorus as presented in Euripides' *Hecuba,* and the fictitious story invented by Tranio in the *Mostellaria.* But Radermacher stresses this point without examining the stories in Pliny and Lucian very carefully. Radermacher also fails to consider the medium of each story: as we shall see, some of his comments on Plautus's *Mostellaria* ignore the fact that its ghost story is told in the context of comic and often frantic action. In other words, generalizations about such stories do not necessarily help us to understand them, and sometimes such generalizations even obscure our understanding.

Radermacher points out an important part of the narrative structure for haunted-house legends when he focuses on the need for a brave man to come on the scene and solve the cause of the haunting. Such a protagonist often appears not only in stories of haunted houses but in other kinds of ghost story as well. We see him in Cicero's tale of the grateful dead man who appeared to Simonides (*Div.* 1.2.7). Since this well-respected poet is sensible enough to accept the advice of the ghost rather than be worried about such a dream or be skeptical about its true nature, the story gains credibility. Another example is the case of the renowned fighter Euthymus, who wrestled with the ghost of Temesa (Paus. 6.6.7–11). Similarly, in the haunted-house stories of Pliny and Lucian, the protagonists are well respected within their social groups. Athenodorus, who faces the ghost in Pliny's story, is a noted Stoic philosopher, and exhibits amazing presence of mind when accosted by the ghost that has terrified so many other people. Lucian introduces the Pythagorean philosopher Arignotos, greatly admired by the group eagerly gathered around him to hear his stories. He does not simply remain calm and wait for the ghost, as Athenodorus does, but actively seeks out the ghost in order to best it. Simonides, Athenodorus, and Arignotos are all highly educated men who are unafraid when facing the unknown. Plautus, in his *Mostellaria,* seems to exploit this traditional type of protagonist: as we shall see, Tranio counts on Theopropides' *not* being such a man, hoping that the presence of a ghost in the house will cause Theopropides to flee in terror.

The tradition of having such a man confront a ghost has lasted for centuries, and a well-known illustration of it occurs in our previous example from *Hamlet,* reflected in the guards' belief that Horatio is the one who ought to confront the ghost of Hamlet's father: "Thou art a scholar; speak to it, Horatio" (1.1.45).[14] In folktales, the theme is developed in the type known as "The Youth Who Wanted to Learn What Fear Is."[15] For haunted houses in particular, the tradition has undergone a noticeable shift in modern times: daring to confront the ghost in a haunted house has become an initiation ritual reserved for adolescents. Teenagers share spooky stories about ghosts or unexplained curses that haunt nearby houses and then visit the houses to test the legends for themselves. This ritual, called a "legend trip" by folklorists, may provide a psychologically safe way for young people to confront anxieties about death.[16] Often the legend trip is part of a fraternity initiation, where a pledge must stay alone in a haunted house for a certain length of time.[17] To succeed, the pledge must exhibit the same qualities Athenodorus had—calmness, good sense, and the ability to reason in the face of the supernatural.

The Haunters and the Haunted—And Their Legal Rights

Another characteristic of haunted-house stories is their tendency to include realistic details. It appears from the surviving classical stories that legal issues involving haunted houses were as debatable in antiquity as they are today. Both then and now, we find three main legal issues concerning haunted houses. The first involves disclosure laws: Do realtors need to inform prospective tenants or owners that a property is allegedly haunted? The second issue is related to disclosure, but has to do with the tenant or owner breaking the lease or contract: Does one who rents or buys property that is haunted, whether or not he knew it was haunted, have legal grounds for refusing to pay rent or mortgage, or for abandoning the property? The third issue is a facetious one, but is nevertheless addressed in ancient and modern haunted-house stories, if not in actual law: Does the *ghost* have any legal rights to the property? For each of these three issues, we can examine modern laws and compare them to what we know or can deduce about such laws in antiquity. What we know for certain about the ancient laws derives mainly from the Roman *Digest* of Justinian. What we can deduce comes from such sources as Cicero's *De officiis* and the few remaining haunted-house stories from antiquity, particularly those found in Plautus's *Mostellaria* and letter 7.27 of Pliny the Younger, which are both Romanized versions of Greek stories. The *Mostellaria* is generally agreed to be based on a Greek comedy, the *Phasma* of Philemon, and, like Pliny's story, takes place in Athens.

On the first issue, disclosure, we find that stories of haunted houses, both ancient and modern, often contain the detail that the rent or selling price of the house was lowered in order to attract tenants. Such a house often has a bad reputation, and the only way for a realtor to unload it is to hope that a great bargain will attract someone who doesn't care—or doesn't know—about the alleged danger.[18] Nowadays, houses with such reputations are called "stigmatized properties"—that is, haunted houses, or homes where notorious crimes have taken place. Other types of stigmatized property include those in which a suicide has occurred, or where someone has died of an illness such as AIDS. Such stigmas do not affect a house physically; they affect it psychologically, and so do not affect the property's appraised value, which is based on comparable houses sold in the same neighborhood. While a stigma should not affect a property's value, it often affects its marketability, by making it harder to sell—or, in some cases, easier to sell. We should also consider a practical explanation for such cases of lowered rent: there is the possibility that tales of haunting are put about by tenants with the intentional aim of keeping the rent down![19]

Certain information is currently protected from disclosure in real-estate transactions—for example, race, handicap, and HIV status of the previous owner. If an agent is asked, he is required by law not to give out that information. But other information, such as alleged hauntings, may or may not be protected from disclosure. Disclosure laws vary from state to state. For example, under North Carolina's disclosure law, realtors are under no obligation to disclose such stigmas unless asked. Real-estate agents there are required by law to disclose only "material facts," information that could affect a property's value. Ghosts, deaths, and serious illnesses are not material facts under North Carolina law; agents do not have to divulge information about them unless directly asked to do so.[20] Under California's disclosure law, sellers of property are required to make full written disclosure of all known material facts that could affect the property's value, including, for example, if the property is on or near an earthquake fault or in a fire-prone area. Unlike North Carolina law, California law does require disclosure of certain deaths on the property: if the death has occurred within the previous three years, it must be disclosed, but if the death occurred more than three years ago, it does not have to be disclosed. The law still raises the questions about which types of death affect a property's value. A murder in the living room ten years ago might be more objectionable to a potential buyer than the fact that a former occupant recently died of old age in the bedroom. The disclosure law does state that sellers must respond honestly to direct questions: if the seller is asked whether anyone died of AIDS in the house, he must disclose the information.[21]

In all, twenty-nine states and the District of Columbia currently require that a buyer be told of *any* problems that might affect a property's value. In states that do not have this requirement, such as North Carolina, many agents feel an ethical responsibility to inform potential buyers anyway, and simply face the consequence that if a house has a bad reputation, it may be difficult to sell. On the other hand, sometimes the rumor of a ghostly inhabitant may *attract* buyers—as in the case of the Hermitage Plantations development in Myrtle Beach, South Carolina, said to be haunted by the ghost of a lovesick young woman.[22]

In states where disclosure of psychological stigmas is required, failure of an agent to do so can result in a lawsuit. For example, in 1989, a New York City man paid $650,000 for a house in Nyack, New York, but learned after the closing that the large old Victorian house had the reputation of being haunted. The buyer then wanted out of his contract, claiming that the real-estate agent had failed to tell him about the ghosts, as required by stigmatized-property disclosure laws, and that he didn't know local lore about the house since he was from out of town. He failed to get the contract overturned at the local level and took the case all the way to the New York Supreme Court. In a 1991 ruling, the Court decided in favor of the buyer, saying his contract was violated because the house "was possessed by poltergeists" and therefore was not vacant at the time of closing! The case led the New York State Association of Realtors to lobby for change in the state law that required buyers to be informed about violent deaths and other aspects of a property that might hurt its value. According to the new law, enacted in 1995, sellers would not have to disclose murders, reports of haunting, etc., unless specifically asked about such instances by a prospective buyer.[23]

In classical antiquity, disclosure issues were apparently quite similar to those we have now, though not as detailed, particularly in reference to psychological factors. Material facts were expected to be disclosed, but apparently were not *required* to be. Cicero, for example, has Diogenes argue that facts should not be withheld from potential buyers (*Off.* 3.13.54):

> Suppose a good man wants to sell a house because of certain flaws, of which he himself is aware, but others are not. The house has an unhealthy atmosphere and they think it is healthy; it is not known that all the bedrooms are infested with snakes; it was poorly built; it is falling apart; but no one other than the owner knows this. I ask you, if the seller does not tell these things to the buyers, and sells the house for more than its worth, hasn't he acted unjustly and dishonestly?[24]

Where material facts were not required to be disclosed, the disclosure of psychological stigmas was not regulated at all. In fact, in antiquity, hauntings were not likely to be considered "psychological stigmas" as they are today, as belief in spirits was not uncommon, though depending on its extent, such a belief could be considered overly superstitious. Pliny's letter, however, contains the suggestion that seeing ghosts *is* the result of a perturbed mind. When the philosopher Athenodorus prepares to spend a night in the haunted house, he concentrates his mind, eyes, and hands on his writing, lest his unoccupied mind imagine it sees the ghost. Pliny's story also includes the detail that the haunted house was advertised at a low rent. Athenodorus, as a potential tenant, finds the low price of the house suspicious. It is an interesting detail, suggesting that haunted houses might in fact have been an economic reality in the ancient world.[25] Evidently realtors in ancient Greece and Rome were not required to inform prospective buyers about any unusual events that had occurred or were still occurring in a house up for rent or sale, unless they were directly asked. Pliny's narrative explains, "The house was deserted and condemned to solitude, and left entirely to the ghost; but it was advertised, in case someone ignorant of the evil might wish to buy or rent it" (7.27.6). But when Athenodorus asks about the reason for the low rent, he is informed about the ghost, and rents the house anyway. While such disclosure was not required, it was evidently an ethical question then as now.[26]

Given the specificity of modern disclosure laws, what then happens if a tenant or owner refuses to pay rent or mortgage, or abandons the property because he believes it to be haunted? In general, as in North Carolina and California law, anyone renting or buying a house with psychological stigmas, whether he knew about them or not, has no legal grounds for refusing to pay rent or mortgage. There is nothing in the ancient law codes that applies specifically to this type of abandonment, but the following passage from the *Digest* of Justinian may have been relevant in the cases of tenants fleeing haunted houses in terror:

> He was asked whether or not someone owes rent if he moved out due to fear. He responded that if there were grounds for his fearing danger, then although there was in fact no danger, he nevertheless owes no rent; but if there was no legally acceptable ground for fear, he still owes it.[27]

The law would be open to debate as to what constituted legally acceptable grounds for fear (*causa timoris iusta*) and what constituted danger (*periculum*). If the walls creaked and the tenant feared the house would collapse, abandonment was probably justified; if the tenant thought the creaking was caused by a ghost, the abandonment was probably *not* justified. But the two crucial terms are left undefined.[28] Not surprisingly, there is no actual case on the books of a tenant being brought to trial for fleeing a house in terror of a ghost. But both Pliny and Plautus provide us with examples of people abandoning or trying to abandon houses for just this reason.

In letter 7.27, Pliny tells us that the chain-rattling ghost of an old man caused the inhabitants of the house to spend terrified sleepless nights there. Many of them even died from terror and lack of sleep. The implication here, as in many haunted-house stories from antiquity on, is that the tenants could not simply leave, as they would then be liable for all the outstanding rent, or they might have been reluctant to give up a substantial investment. (And, of course, if they left right away, there wouldn't be much of a story.) But eventually the house is deserted and abandoned to the ghost, and an indefinite period of time passes before Athenodorus decides to rent the place.

The issue in the *Mostellaria* is more complicated. The ghost story in the play is invented by the slave Tranio to keep his master Theopropides away from the house. Theopropides, the miserly father of the young Philolaches, has returned home unexpectedly, and Tranio wants to keep from him the knowledge of his son's extravagant parties. Playing on the old man's superstitious nature, Tranio informs him that his son has moved out because the house is haunted. The ghost claims the house as his dwelling because the former owner killed him and hid the body on the premises. Having died violently and before his time, and without proper burial, the murdered man could not be received into Hades. While many ghosts in Greek and Roman ghost stories haunt because they did not receive proper burial and their spirits cannot rest, the ghost invented by Tranio doesn't care about proper burial. Instead, the ghost claims squatter's rights, saying, "Here I dwell, this place has been given to me as a home" (498, 504), and orders Theopropides, the legal owner, out of the house with the command "Emigra!" ("Leave!" 503). Among other things, there may be an allusion here to justifiable abandonment of property by a tenant: the usual word for tenant abandonment is *migrare,* that is, "to change residences." [29] And in the passage from the *Digest* given above, the technical term for tenant abandonment is *emigrare.* Meanwhile, the inconsistency involved in the ghost's failure to ask for burial arises as part of Tranio's trick: the whole point is to get the owner to abandon the house, and so the continuance of the ghostly inhabitant is necessary to Tranio's story. If the ghost simply wanted a proper burial, the owner could perform the rites, clear the house, and move back in.

The idea of a ghost's establishing itself in a house rather than wanting proper burial was popular enough to last over the centuries, reappearing, for example, in the story of the Amityville Horror:

> The priest . . . entered the house to begin his ritual of blessing. When he flicked the first holy water and uttered the words that accompany the gesture, Father Mancuso heard a masculine voice say with terrible clarity: "*Get out!*" He looked up in shock and whirled about. . . . The command had come from directly behind him, but he was alone in the room. Who or whatever had spoken was nowhere to be seen! [30]

Science-fiction writers Isaac Asimov and Frederic Pohl, in a departure from their usual genre, take up the problem of a ghost's legal claim to a house in their story "Legal Rites." The obnoxious human heir to a property finds that a ghost who was his father's friend is claiming squatter's rights. "Get off my land," a disembodied voice says to the heir, who promptly brings suit against the intruder. The ghost, successfully persuading a lawyer to defend him, says, "The fact that I was once killed by violence, and have to continue my existence on the astral plane, doesn't mean I've lost my legal rights— does it?" In the courtroom, the defending lawyer opens his argument by saying, "Your honor, we propose to show that my client, by virtue of a sustained residence of more than twenty years in the house located on Route 22, has acquired certain rights. In legal terminology we define these as the rights of adverse possession. The layman would call them common-law rights—squatter's rights." To the dismay of the plaintiff, the judge rules in favor of the ghost.[31]

To sum up, what we know about ancient and modern legal issues in-volving haunted houses is largely consistent. Regarding disclosure, both an-cient and modern laws seem to be in agreement that the alleged presence of ghosts need not be mentioned to a prospective tenant or buyer. Both then and now, it was an ethical question rather than a legal one. The issue of refusal to pay rent or mortgage, or of abandoning the property due to fear of ghosts, has been more of a legal concern (naturally, since money is involved). The facetious question of whether the ghost has any legal rights is not a legitimate legal concern, but the popularity of the theme forces us to notice that in spite of the sacred and binding rite of proper burial, so important to both the Greeks and the Romans, the possibility was left open that not all restless spirits would seek proper burial. Some want to retain possession of the houses they haunt. Finally, although it is difficult to know whether the lawcourts in Greece and Rome would ever have had occasion to deal with these issues, in cases analogous to those in Plautus and Pliny, the owner or renter of such a house might have had recourse to a tribunal in order to obtain some resolution about the contract.[32] Ultimately, how-ever, it is important to remember that what we are observing in these stories is basically the intrusion of technical legal detail upon what in most other respects is essentially folkloric material.

Keeping in mind the characteristics of haunted houses and the accom-panying ghost-lore, we can now turn our attention to the surviving stories of Plautus, Pliny, and Lucian. Unlike so many other supernatural beings in antiquity, such as the warning apparitions, the ghosts found in these stories are not considered omens or portents. Rather, they are the restless dead, in need of a proper burial, and their appearances are attended by many of the characteristics discussed in previous chapters. For example, although they all appear at night, to people in various states of consciousness, one of them speaks while the other two do not, and their descriptions vary from the black color discussed by Winkler to the emaciated, ragged ghost of an old man in chains. We can observe the working of Radermacher's archetype to see what each author has done with the narrative structure, and especially with the character of the protagonist. As we shall see, whereas Pliny gives us the archetype of the calm, educated man, Plautus's comedy functions effectively in the *absence* of such a rational protagonist, and Lucian's satire is based on the exaggeration of a scholar dealing with the supernatural.

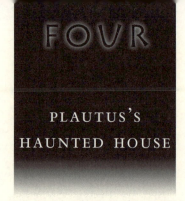

FOUR

PLAUTUS'S HAUNTED HOUSE

IN THE *MOSTELLARIA* OF THE ROMAN COMIC PLAYWRIGHT PLAUTUS, we have the earliest extant haunted-house story in Greek and Roman literature.[1] Fragments of late Greek comedies tell us that there were several plays titled *Phasma,* or "The Ghost," including one by the popular comedian Philemon, who died in 262 B.C. It was probably Philemon's play that Plautus adapted nearly three-quarters of a century later for the *Mostellaria.*[2] The ghost story invented in the play by the slave character Tranio has been regularly accepted as a traditional haunted-house story, of the kind told by Pliny in letter 7.27 and satirized by Lucian in his Philopseudes (30–31).[3] The story, told not quite halfway into the play, forms part of an attempt to prevent the miserly old man Theopropides from finding out the truth about his son's extravagant expenses, and its effectiveness would have depended in part on the audience's familiarity with haunted-house stories. But a closer look at the story in the *Mostellaria,* based on comparison with what we know about such stories in antiquity, shows that it is the deviations from conventional details, and not simply Tranio's deception, that motivate the rest of the play's action. Tranio's story "has all the characteristics of a yarn that is being made up as it proceeds—hesitancy, much irrelevant detail, inconsistency, vagueness."[4] More traditional ghost stories, with which the audience would have been familiar, most likely had fewer or no inconsistencies. Plautus's audience would consequently see Tranio's deviations from convention not only as deviations from a familiar genre, but as logical problems and, more importantly, as Plautus's way of characterizing Tranio and creating dramatic tension. Will Theopropides see through Tranio's ruse, or will he be overwhelmed by Tranio's dramatic delivery during the story? Comparison of this ghost story with others from antiquity helps to account for the inconsistencies in Tranio's story and their effects, both immediate and consequent, on the action of the play.

The Ghost Story in the *Mostellaria*

The ghost story in the play, as constructed by Plautus for the slave Tranio, is entirely fictitious. It contains many of the motifs common to haunted-house stories. Tranio invents the story to keep his master Theopropides away from the house. Theopropides, the miserly father of the young Philo-laches, has returned home unexpectedly early from a business trip abroad, and Tranio wants to keep the old man from finding out about his son's misbehavior[5]—largely because Tranio himself has had a part in the mis-management of the household. He shuts Philolaches and his friends in the house, and then, playing on Theopropides' superstitious nature, informs him that his son has moved out because the house is haunted. In the follow-ing scene, Tranio comes up with the rather complicated—and muddled—story:

TR. I tell you, a crime has been committed—an old crime, committed long ago.

TH. Long ago?

TR. We have only recently found out about it.

TH. Well, what is this crime? And who committed it? I'm listening.

TR. A host murdered his own guest, taking him by force. If you ask me, it was that very same man who sold you this house!

TH. Murdered him?

TR. Yes, and stole his gold. And then he buried the man—his guest—here in this very house.

TH. How did you find out about all of this?

TR. Listen, I'll tell you. Your son had dined out, and after he returned home from dinner, we all went to bed. We were sleeping; I hap-pened to have forgotten to put out the lamp; and suddenly he cried out very loudly!

TH. Who cried out? My son?

TR. Quiet! Just listen for a minute! He said that a dead man had come to him in his sleep.

TH. Really—in his sleep?

TR. Yes. But just listen: he said that the dead man spoke to him in this way—

TH. In his sleep?

TR. Yes! It would have been amazing if the dead man had spoken to him while he was awake, seeing as how the fellow had already been dead for sixty years. You are awfully stupid!

TH. I'll be quiet.

TR. Just hear what the dead man said to him: "I am a visiting traveler from across the sea, Diapontius by name. Here I dwell; this place has been given to me as a home. For Orcus refused to accept me into the Land of the Dead, because I lost my life prematurely. I was too trusting: my host killed me here, and he buried me secretly, without the proper rites, here on these premises, a criminal act, for the sake of gold. Now leave this place! This building is cursed, this dwelling is polluted by crime." It would take more than a year to tell you what prodigies have been seen here![6]

This appears, on the surface, to be a typical haunted-house story. The house has a bad reputation, here referred to not only by the word *impia* but by the several repetitions of the word *scelus* and its variants. The house acquired this bad reputation for two reasons. First, a terrible crime was committed there, with the date specified as about sixty years earlier: the previous owner killed his own guest, stole his gold, and buried the body on the premises. Second, the ghost of the murdered guest now haunts the place. There, however, the similarities to other stories end. Tranio's story contains several loopholes and inconsistencies, both because he has to make it up on the spur of the moment and because Theopropides keeps interrupting him. Plautus, as we shall see, uses these loopholes as dramatic devices. Though we do not know how much Plautus relied on a specific Greek model for his story, we can see that several of the elements of Diapontius's story are based in Greek tragedy, and must have made their way through New Comedy to its Latin imitators.

Themes from Tragedy

Although the essence of the haunted-house story is based on folkloric tradition, Tranio in his fictitious story has also used a theme from tragedy: a ghost reveals the crime that has been committed against him.[7] Although "the degree to which Plautus is parodying a specific play, rather than the concept of stage tragedy in general, is not clear,"[8] there are at least two tragedies in which the ghost of a murdered man returns to tell of his murder, as Diapontius does here. The first is Euripides' *Hecuba,* in which the ghost of Polydorus actually delivers the prologue. He has come to the camp of the Achaeans specifically to make his mother Hecuba aware of his fate: he was killed by his host, Polymestor, who coveted his gold. He has returned to beseech his mother to perform the rites of burial for him so that he may find peace among the dead, because as long as his body lies unburied on the shore or is tossed in the sea, his spirit is doomed to restless wandering (*Hec.* 25–30):

My host, friend of my father (ξένος πατρῷος), killed me (κτείνει με), unfortunate that I am, for the sake of gold (χρυσοῦ . . . χάριν), and then threw me into the surging sea, so that he could keep the gold for himself. My body lies neglected on the shore, then drifts out to sea again, borne with the tide's ebb and flow, unmourned, unburied (ἄταφος).[9]

Several phrases from Tranio's story reflect themes from the Greek, which suggests that Plautus (or his Greek model) had the Polydorus story in mind, if not Euripides' play in particular.[10] Plautus's *hospes me necavit* ("my host killed me") echoes κτείνει με . . . ξένος πατρῷος, both embodying the concept of violated guest-friendship. The Latin construction *auri causa* ("for the sake of gold") parallels χρυσοῦ . . . χάριν, while *insepultum* ("unburied" or "buried without the proper rites") translates ἄταφος.[11] And although Diapontius's body was not left tossing in the waves, the repetition of *transmarinus* ("across the sea") and its Greek counterpart *Diapontius* does evoke sea imagery.[12]

The second tragedy from which Plautus could have drawn is Pacuvius's *Iliona,* which is essentially the Polydorus story with a slight twist. Iliona, Polydorus's sister, has substituted her own son Deiphilus for Polydorus, and her husband Polymestor kills Deiphilus by mistake.[13] Like Polydorus in Euripides' *Hecuba,* Deiphilus's shade begs for burial; unlike Polydorus, Deiphilus's ghost appears to his mother in her sleep—though in this play, the ghost actually comes onto the stage. A few of the ghost's lines remain: "Mother, I call you, who ease your distress with soft slumber / and feel no pity for me; rise and bury your son! . . . And do not, I beg you, let my wretched remains with their bared bones be stained with stinking gore and dragged along the ground."[14] It is interesting to note that although Iliona's inexcusable deception had really been the cause of Deiphilus's death, the portion of his speech remaining to us contains no hint that he desires revenge.[15]

Diapontius's "tragic" situation parallels that of Polydorus and Deiphilus. Tranio gives Diapontius's speech tragic features, including, for example, the repetition of a concept phrased in two slightly different ways: *hic habito, haec mihi dedita est habitatio* ("Here I dwell; this place has been given to me as a home," 498), and *scelestae hae sunt aedes, impia est habitatio* ("This building is cursed, this dwelling is polluted by crime," 504).[16] Such repetition is frequent in tragedy,[17] and the word *habitatio* itself is an elevated expression, used by Plautus only in this passage and at the end of a line of *Trinummus,* where it is part of a solemn invocation to a god. Furthermore, long words at the end of a verse are among the features that heighten the tone of Latin tragedy and epic.[18] Like the tragedians, Tranio is trying to terrify his audience—at least, the part of the audience not in on the joke, that is, Theopropides. Tranio makes the ghost even more effective by implying that he is a merchant like Theopropides: Diapontius underwent the same risks during his life as does Theopropides now in traveling overseas and in trusting gods and hosts. The emphasis on gold is a detail Theopropides could be expected to notice.

Tranio continues to work on Theopropides psychologically by referring to the ghost as *mortuus* ("a dead man"), a word usually applied not to ghosts but to corpses. Whereas words such as *larva* and *lemures* were certainly also terrifying, Plautus may have Tranio use *mortuus* in order to continue the theme that has already been running through the conversation: death. The death of an inconvenient wife, parent, or master is hoped for regularly in comedy as the easiest way of preventing that person's interference.[19] Although no one is ever really killed in comedy, a character like Tranio is allowed to kill his annoying master in word rather than in deed. Before Theopropides' entrance, Tranio warms to the idea of having some fun with the old man, saying, "Today I will play some games with this old man, while he's alive, which, I'm sure, he would never experience when he's dead" (*ludos ego hodie vivo praesenti hic seni / faciam, quod credo mortuo numquam fore*, 427–28). Duckworth notes the play on *ludos*, a word that means both "sport" and "funeral games."[20] When Theopropides comes on the scene, returning from overseas, he refers to his narrow escape from the dangerous sea: "Neptune, thanks so much for delivering me to my house barely alive" (*habeo, Neptune, gratiam magnam tibi, / quom med amisisti a te vix vivom domum*, 431–32). Tranio, in an aside to the audience, announces his disappointment that Neptune did not take advantage of having the old man in his power.[21] And when Theopropides says that the household must be eagerly awaiting his return, Tranio mutters, "By God, that man would be more eagerly awaited who came to announce that you had died" (*nimio edepol ille potuit exspectatior / venire qui te nuntiaret mortuom*, 442–43). Tranio demonstrates a preoccupation with the idea of a dead man. Although Theopropides has not died, the constant references to death probably provide Tranio with the theme for his story and with his subsequent use of the word *mortuus* for the ghost, rather than one of the many words for "apparition." The word also carries a tacit threat to Theopropides: he may end up like Diapontius if he isn't careful.

Several changes in the details of the story set Tranio's tale apart from the versions of Euripides and Pacuvius. In switching the character from the Trojan Polydorus to Diapontius, Tranio has not only drawn a parallel with

Theopropides, but has also changed the story from heroic legend to fiction set in the everyday world (this is one of the goals of comedic adaptation in general). Moving the setting of the story from the Greek camp of Euripides' *Hecuba* or the royal palace of Pacuvius's *Iliona* to a house in Athens also removes the story from the mythical past. Unfortunately for Tranio, his hastily improvised story contains many inconsistencies, and his ability to cover for them in the face of Theopropides' continuous skepticism provides much comic tension. Only some of these inconsistencies have been noted by commentators, and a comparison of Tranio's story with other ghost stories from antiquity shows more specifically just how poor a liar Tranio is.

Anomalies in the Haunted-House Plot

As Tranio begins setting the scene for his story, he explains that Philolaches had this dream after falling asleep with the light on. Tranio says, "I happened to have forgotten to put out the lamp" (487). Why mention this strange detail? The flustered slave is stalling for time, has been frequently interrupted, and is not entirely coherent. But it is worth noting that in the two other most detailed haunted-house stories from antiquity, those of Pliny and Lucian, it is also clearly stated that a lamp was shining. In those stories, the lamp is ostensibly present because the philosophers need the light to work by, but the detail also suggests that in haunted-house stories from antiquity, a lighted lamp needed to be present for a ghost to appear. As discussed in Chapter 1, lamps were commonly found in graves, following the tradition that torches and lamps were carried in funeral processions to light the way for the dead on their journey to the next world.[22] The lost souls who haunt houses were thought to be drawn by the light, which they hoped would show them the way out of their predicament. Another explanation for the presence of lamps in these stories arises from what we know about descriptions of ghosts in antiquity. Ghosts in Greece and Rome were not thought of as luminous, as they often are today, where turning on a light is more likely to cause a ghost to disappear. Rather, ghosts in antiquity, as we have seen, were sometimes described as white, sometimes as black or smoky, like soot from the pyre, and sometimes simply as having the appearance that the person had when alive. In other words, the light would have been necessary simply in order to be able to see the ghost. The problem is that this makes sense *only if the ghost were appearing in person*, rather than in a dream.[23] There are no other instances of dream-ghosts appearing by lamplight; Patroclus did not appear to Achilles by lamplight, for example, and in the stories of dream-ghosts cited from Apuleius there is no mention of the sleepers having left the light on (*Met.* 8.8–9, 9.31). In this part of his story, Tranio in his haste seems to have conflated two different types of ghost-lore.

There are additional problems connected with the ghost's appearance in Philolaches' dream.[24] Whereas in many types of ghost story, the ghost might appear in a dream, it seems this was not the case with haunted-house stories, where the main point was that the ghost had a physical presence and the house had to be cleared—as in Pliny and Lucian, for example, as well as in the shorter stories of haunted places we have seen from Suetonius and Pausanias.[25] This may be because dream-ghosts were not considered to be haunting a person or a place. They generally came to warn or advise or ask for help, but were not bound to the place where they died and never constituted a personal threat to the safety of the inhabitants. They certainly never claimed squatter's rights, as Diapontius does here.[26] Tranio's story deviates from convention on this point, which causes problems immediately as Theopropides, finding it less than remarkable that his son should have a mere dream about a ghost, requests confirmation of this detail (490–93). There is some dispute about whether *nempe* ("really") has an entirely ironic meaning in line 491 (*nempe ergo in somnis?*), or whether Theopropides is just trying to clarify the facts.[27] He certainly seems to be having trouble grasping the obvious; two lines earlier, when Tranio explains that Philolaches cried out in his sleep, Theopropides seems unnecessarily confused ("Who cried out? My son?" 489).[28] But this exchange also contains the implication that the ghost would have been more terrifying had it appeared in person, and Theopropides seems to feel let down after the big buildup about the murdered man. This is not to say that dream-ghosts could not also be terrifying; the gory examples discussed in Chapter 1 must have been more than disconcerting to the dreamers. But here Tranio has to compensate for Theopropides' surprising lack of concern with the less-than-convincing argument that the murdered man could not possibly appear in person, since he had already been dead for sixty years (493–94).

Surely Tranio is not implying in these lines that ghosts can appear *only* in dreams; there is no precedent for this, particularly with a long tradition in both tragedy and comedy of stage ghosts appearing to people who are wide awake. And there seems to be yet another inconsistency here: ghosts appearing in dreams are most frequently the apparitions of the recently deceased, not of people who have already been dead for decades. But the opposition of *in somnis* ("in his sleep") and *vigilanti* ("awake") in the same line (493) suggests that Tranio may be counting on Theopropides' confusion to convince him that a ghost could not possibly appear in person.

Tranio successfully confuses Theopropides even more by saying—presumably with some exasperation—"You are awfully stupid!" (495). The irony here is that Theopropides is in fact smart to question Tranio's story, but Tranio must get the old man to be stupid so that he will believe the lie. At the very least, Tranio tries to use sarcasm to convince the old man that the ghost could not speak unless it appeared in a dream, which suggests that ghosts who had something to communicate generally did so through dreams rather than by appearing to someone who was awake.[29] For the moment, Tranio has muddled his details, and it is only by what must be an exasperated and insistent delivery of these lines that he can convince Theopropides that the ghost really is a threat.

Tranio's need for his fictitious ghost to tell its story causes more problems, however, as the hastily invented ghost story contains two very large loopholes when Tranio deviates from convention again. The first loophole comes when Tranio has the ghost say that he was murdered by the previous owner of the house and improperly buried *on the premises*. This careless detail ignores the more traditional ending of these stories: once you know a body is buried on the premises, you have only to dig it up and give it a proper burial, which allows the troubled spirit to rest, putting an end to the haunting. The problem may be exacerbated by Tranio's allowing the ghost to say, "Orcus refused to accept me into the Land of the Dead, because I lost my life prematurely."[30] On the one hand, the *biaiothanatoi* (victims of violent deaths) and *ataphoi* (unburied) were thought to be especially dangerous, and the phrase is probably intended to terrify Theopropides. On the other hand, all Theopropides would have to do to ruin Tranio's deception is point out that the body needs a proper burial. There would, of course, be no body to find, which Tranio would have to admit if people started prying up the floor-tiles and digging in the yard in search of a corpse. The success of the story depends on an inspired delivery by Tranio, one that keeps Theopropides from having time to think.

This particular inconsistency in Tranio's story has drawn much unnecessary criticism. Ziegler says, "Tranio should avoid making statements which can easily be checked," but admits that he covers it well with his insistence on how dangerous the house is.[31] Wieand, in her discussion of deception in Plautus, suggests that Plautus could easily have avoided the inconsistencies, but must not have cared to (Wieand doesn't explain why).[32] Radermacher objects strenuously to Plautus's having Tranio invent such a story, considering it extremely clumsy of the playwright to have left such a loophole. Plautus, he explains, must have known the usual ending for haunted-house stories, or he would not have let Tranio explain that the dead houseguest was lying buried in the house itself. But it was very careless of Plautus to include this detail, he says, because it raises the question of why nobody had long since arranged for a proper burial and for purification of the house—or of why there were no earlier rumors of a haunting.[33]

Radermacher's objections, however, fail to consider several points. In the first place, the audience might have had the same objections: they would most probably have been familiar with the traditional resolution for such cases (discovery and burial of the body) and might have been wondering whether Theopropides would bring up this point, particularly since the old man seems less worried when he hears that the ghost appeared in a dream. By using such a distorted story, then, Plautus intended to create humorous suspense for the audience. In the second place, it is equally possible that neither the audience nor Theopropides would have had time to think about that loophole, given what was probably an inspired and frantic presentation by Tranio, who constantly distracts Theopropides with repeated admonitions of "Listen!" (*ausculta*). We can imagine Tranio speaking eerily as he gives the background to his story, and then switching to a different, ominous, threatening voice as he recounts the ghost's dream-speech. The long vowel sounds in many of the words in this speech could easily be drawn out to sound like the moaning and groaning of a tortured spirit (e.g., *habito, Orcus, careo, defodit, scelestae hae . . . aedes*). The last two lines of the ghost's speech, with the command *emigra* delivered in the proper ominous tone, would not leave Theopropides in a state for clear thinking.[34] Tranio has the ghost emphasize—with the repetitions of *hic, haec, hisce,* and *hae*—that the house belongs to him; and it is important that this particular ghost, unlike Polydorus and Deiphilus, is not requesting burial. The loophole, then, for several reasons, might have escaped the notice of both Theopropides and the audience, or at least might not have concerned them to the extent that it has bothered modern critics.

The other major flaw in Tranio's story is that the previous owner of the house is alive and still residing in the neighborhood. The danger here is that Theopropides could speak with him—which he promptly does, in the very next scene: "I'm going to visit the man I bought the house from" (547). This nearly ruins Tranio's plan. Tranio has to convince Theopropides that the previous owner is a liar: of course the man is not going to admit to a murder (*negat scelestus,* "The criminal denies it," 554)! But Theopropides is not easily convinced, and for a while things begin to look bad for Tranio. Luckily for him, this dangerous conversation is interrupted and, strangely enough, the subject of the previous owner is dropped for the rest of the play. Another problem concerning the previous owner is the inconsistency in Tranio's use of *sexaginta annos*. The number is not normally used indefinitely in phrases to mean "many years" as opposed to exactly "sixty," but if it is not being used indefinitely here, it would suggest that the former owner of Theopropides' house is at least eighty years old, which seems unlikely, and is something Theopropides might have picked up on if he had been paying attention.[35] While Tranio himself is most likely confused at this point in his story, the detail also shows how well Tranio has managed to confuse Theopropides, underlining the progress of the reversal that has occurred in the master/slave relationship.

This leaves one other odd inconsistency in Tranio's story, the one by which Theopropides finally learns the truth and realizes just how badly he was taken in. This is the knocking on the door, which supposedly disturbs the ghost. While insistent knocking on the door was a typical scene in the *comoedia palliata*,[36] Plautus here uses it for a different effect. As noted earlier, Tranio had first alarmed Theopropides by yelling at him not to knock on the door, or even to touch the house, because it might disturb the ghost (445–62). Tranio attempts to play on Theopropides' superstitious nature by telling him that in touching the door of the alleged haunted house, he has committed murder (463–65):

TR.   By God, you've killed—
TH.   I've killed whom?
TR.   Your whole family!
TH.   May the gods and goddesses take you and your omen and—
TR.   I fear that you may not be able to purify yourself and them![37]

A mention of death in one's family was especially ominous to one returning from a journey, and for Theopropides this does not bode well.[38] At this point, however, the old man is more irritable than superstitious, and Tranio has to put in some effort to convince him of the danger. But when Philolaches and his friends inside the house start making noises, Tranio's deception almost fails: "I'm done for," he says in an aside; "soon they will destroy my story!" (510).[39] He has to say that it is the ghost knocking back in response to Theopropides. This implies that the ghost, though it appeared in a dream, does have a physical manifestation, confusing Theopropides even more. In addition to the knocking, we also have Tranio's claim that *monstra* were seen in the house. This remains quite vague, as Tranio leaves the particular kinds of portent to our imagination.[40] Yet the *monstra* hint again at physical manifestations of the spirit disturbing the house. In the extant ghost stories from antiquity, however, ghosts generally appear either in dreams or in person, not in both, and it would be highly unusual for Diapontius, who appeared in a dream, to present himself to the waking inhabitants of the house.

To add to this problem, Tranio's claim that a ghost causes the knocking sounds may be our earliest evidence for belief in poltergeist-type hauntings. If the audience had been familiar with such supernatural activity, the humor of the scene would have been richer, and Theopropides' near-panic would have needed no explanation. Another point to consider is that this knocking provides an emphasis on the sounds caused by the ghost rather than on its physical appearance, which is something that occurs in Pliny's haunted-house story as well. Tranio does not physically describe the ghost at all, though he gives it a name and a background. The lack of description implies that the mere idea of a ghost, at least to someone as superstitious as Theopropides, was enough to evoke terror. In any case, it is not until Theopropides finds the slaves Pinacium and Phaniscus pounding on the door of the allegedly haunted house that he learns the truth, and the resolution of the play begins (935ff.). The slaves tell him that the noises have been caused by Philolaches and his friends having wild parties the whole time.[41]

When we compare these details from Tranio's story with those of other ancient ghost stories, we realize how mangled Tranio's invention is. Although earlier in the play he had been thinking of a way to deceive Theopropides (388ff.), he had not worked out a plan or decided on a clear course of action.[42] He was trying to think of a way not only to prevent the old man from entering the house but also to cause him to flee the house in fear. This is evidenced at lines 389–90, when he tries to reassure Philolaches: "Will you be satisfied if I bring it about that your father will not only not enter the house when he arrives, but will flee far from it?" And again at 423–24, speaking to a slave: "I will bring it about that he will not only not dare to look in the house, but will flee with his head covered in terror!"[43] Wieand concludes that Tranio's artful trickery and clear superiority have resulted in a masterful deception of Theopropides,[44] presumably by way of a skilled rhetorical display. In Tranio, however, Plautus has intentionally created a most inefficient kind of oral storyteller: one who does not work well under pressure from an audience (in this case, Theopropides). His story, hastily improvised and frantically delivered, contains more than the usual number of flaws we might expect from the stock character of the "Clever Slave" (*servus callidus*) and is not the entirely cunning deception suggested by Sutton.[45]

The success of Tranio's story, in fact, depends not so much on his own cleverness as on Theopropides' gullibility and superstitious nature. The story would have been a failure from the start if not for the improbable situation—which does not occur in other haunted-house stories—of Theopropides' somehow never having heard a story so closely connected to his own house. Theopropides is probably the most striking example of the "gullible old man" (*credulus senex*) in Plautus,[46] since Tranio dupes him so completely, even with such a muddled story. Theopropides, in his willingness to believe such an inconsistent and unsupportable story, shows some of the characteristics of Theophrastus's *deisidaimon,* who "will not tread upon a tombstone, or come near a dead body."[47] We have seen how Tranio tried to play on the old man's superstitious beliefs by telling him that he would never be able to purify himself after knocking on the door. Although Theopropides initially shows some skepticism, he is soon convinced to keep his distance from the house, which is polluted by murder ("scelestae hae sunt aedes, impia est habitatio," 504), and contains a dead body. The *deisidaimon,* who avoided tombs, also refused to pay the last rites to the dead.[48] This consideration, too, would lessen the inconsistency of having the body on the premises. And so, instead of saying that the comic effects of this ghost story on the plot of the *Mostellaria* arise simply from Tranio's clever deception, we have to admit that Theopropides' stupidity and superstitious nature are largely responsible for the comedy, and that his confusion arises not from traditional elements in haunted-house stories, but from distortions of them.

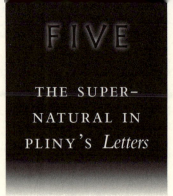

THE SUPER-
NATURAL IN
PLINY'S *Letters*

PROBABLY THE MOST FAMOUS GHOST STORIES FROM ANTIQUITY ARE those that survive in the letters of Pliny the Younger, which were published between A.D. 100 and 109. The letters cover a wide variety of subjects—politics, social events, family life, science. Occasionally Pliny wrote about the supernatural, and in letter 7.27 he discusses the nature of apparitions. In the letter, addressed to his friend Lucius Licinius Sura,[1] Pliny inquires whether Sura believes there really are such things as ghosts and what their nature might be (7.27.1): "I should very much like to know whether you think there are such things as ghosts, and whether they have their own shapes and some divine existence, or whether they are unreal images that take their forms from our own anxieties."[2] The inquiry implies a certain amount of skepticism on Pliny's part by suggesting that apparitions are products of the imagination, which conforms to the Epicurean view we have seen expressed, for example, in Plutarch (*Brut.* 37.1–3). That Pliny brings up the subject implies that stories such as these were circulating regularly in society. Although Pliny does not specify his sources, several characteristics in his retellings point to an oral tradition for the stories. Yet by asking Sura his opinion, Pliny also implies that Sura might not have heard these particular stories before.

To a certain extent, these implications may be due only to the formal rhetorical structure of the letter. Using a familiar pattern, Pliny follows his opening inquiry with three examples.[3] The first story is a short one about Curtius Rufus and his vision of the superhuman woman who claims to be the representation of Africa (discussed in Chapter 2). She foretells his future as the governor of that province, and the incident is interpreted as a personal omen for Curtius Rufus. Clearly this story was circulating in society, being passed along via an oral tradition, as we find it also in Tacitus (*Ann.* 11.21), and Pliny himself says, "I hear that this happened to Curtius Rufus" (*audio accidisse Curtio Rufo,* 7.27.2). Rufus owed his various promotions to the emperor Tiberius, so the story must have been an old one by Pliny's time. The second and best-known story, which will be discussed in detail below, is set in Athens and may also come from an oral tradition. But the third story in letter 7.27 takes place in Pliny's own household.

The Mystery of the Phantom Barbers

The third story concerns two of Pliny's servants: they had visions of apparitions who cut their hair off, and the servants woke in the morning with their hair actually shorn. Pliny heard this story directly from them and consequently gives it some credence, interpreting it as a personal omen for himself:

> I have a freedman with some education. He was sleeping in the same bed as his younger brother. This younger brother thought he saw a certain man sitting by the bed, moving a razor toward his head, and actually cutting hairs from the very top of his head. When the sun came up, this younger brother was shorn around the top of his head, and the hairs were found lying on the floor. After a short time, a similar incident gave credit to the previous one. A slave-boy was sleeping in the common area with the other slave-boys. There came through the windows (so he says), in white shirts, two men, who gave the sleeping boy a haircut and left by the same way they had entered. Once again, daylight showed that the boy's head was shorn, and that the cut hairs were scattered around. Nothing of note happened next, unless it was that by chance I was not called to court as a defendant, which I would surely have been, if Domitian, under whom these incidents occurred, had lived longer. For a short letter against me was found in Carus's writing-box, from which it can be supposed that, because it is the custom of defendants to let their hair grow long, the cutting of my servants' hair was a sign that the danger that threatened me had been averted.[4]

Carus, one of Domitian's informers and a personal enemy of Pliny, probably wanted to get Pliny out of the way.[5] But in spite of whatever evidence against Pliny was in that letter Carus had written, Pliny was not accused of anything and was not called to court.

Pliny takes the servant's dream in this story rather seriously, saying, "I can affirm the story to others" (*illud adfirmare aliis possum*), because it happened to his own servants. Most commentators, however, think that Pliny somehow didn't realize a joke was being played on him. Russell suspects that Pliny's servants were simply kidding around: "The idea of a practical joke, or an attempt by his servants to cheer him up, never occurred to him."[6] Merrill wonders why the omen should have been sent to Pliny's slave rather than to himself, while Sherwin-White points out that the portents affected Pliny himself because the boys were his own property.[7]

Merrill also wonders why the simplest interpretation here was not that of contraries, meaning that the cutting of the hair indicated that Pliny's throat would not be cut.[8] There was an ancient folk-belief that some dreams were to be interpreted by contraries; for example, to be beaten or killed sometimes portended good luck.[9] Pliny himself had advocated interpretation of dreams by contraries, as we see from his advice to the historian/biographer Suetonius in letter 1.18.2–4. Suetonius had had an upsetting dream that he feared was an ill omen for a law case he was involved in. He wondered whether to request a postponement, and asked Pliny's opinion. Pliny replied:

> It makes a difference whether you are accustomed to dreaming things that eventually come to pass, or whether things turn out contrary to what you dream. When I consider a dream of my own, that dream which you fear seems to me to portend a successful outcome for you. I had taken up the case of Junius Pater, when my mother-in-law appeared to me in my sleep, and, falling to her knees before me, begged me not to take the case. I was at the time a young man just starting on my career; the case was going before the Four Courts; I was going up against the most powerful men in the State—they were even friends of the emperor.[10] Each of these facts individually was enough to discourage me after such an upsetting dream. I took the case anyway, considering that "the best omen is to fight for one's country":[11] for loyalty toward a client seemed to me as dear as my country, or dearer, if possible. As it turned out, I won the case, and what's more, that lawsuit brought me good publicity and opened the door to fame.[12]

Pliny's decision to go forward with the case may have had more to do with his attitude toward his mother-in-law than with any strong belief about interpretation by contraries.[13] Overall, Pliny shows no consistency in his interpretation of dreams, but as he advises Suetonius, "Consider whether you, too, based on this example, might turn that dream you had to your advantage" (*dispice, an tu quoque sub hoc exemplo somnium istud in bonum vertas,* 1.18.5). He seems content simply to interpret dreams favorably no matter how much he might have to distort them to do so. The dreams reported by the slaves were certainly specific, including scissor-bearing apparitions, and the corroborating evidence of cut hair lying strewn about the room. This material evidence, and the fact that the alleged apparitions had to climb in and out of a window, suggest that the occurrences were indeed no dreams, but Pliny doesn't seriously consider that the incidents might have actually happened,[14] despite his parenthetical comment "So he says" (*ita narrat,* 7.27.13), which seems to express a trace of skepticism.

The Haunted House at Athens

After Plautus's *Mostellaria,* the next extant description of a haunted house in ancient literature is found nearly three centuries later, in this same letter of Pliny. The second and longest ghost story from letter 7.27 is probably the single most famous ghost story from antiquity. It contains many of the characteristics of migratory legends (discussed in Chapter 1). It has a real setting, Athens; it takes place in the past, but not the remote past of heroic-age legend; the protagonist may be a real person, a "friend of a friend," which adds some credibility to the tale; the story is told by a person of some education; and the timing and order of events indicate an awareness of literary form. We do not know where Pliny heard the story, but it is clear that he did hear it as opposed to reading it somewhere: "I will tell it as I heard it" (*exponam ut accepi,* 7.27.4), he writes to Sura. There are other indications in Pliny's letter that this story was circulating orally before he recorded it. The story contains many sound effects but few physical descriptions, and the phrase "if you listened" (*si attenderes,* 7.27.5) seems to allude to a wider audience: this sudden shift from a third-person narrative to a direct address in the second person was almost certainly not directed at Sura, the recipient of this letter. The story in many ways also preserves what might be considered an archetypical narrative structure of the haunted-house legend, maintaining the essential plot laid out by Radermacher. Someone has been killed and buried on the grounds; the spirit of the deceased walks at night, until a courageous man discovers the cause of the haunting; when the mortal remains are properly buried, tranquility returns to the house.

> In Athens there was a large and roomy house, but it had a bad reputation and an unhealthy air. Through the silence of the night you could hear the sound of metal clashing and, if you listened more closely, you could make out the clanking of chains, first from far off, then from close by. Soon there appeared a phantom, an old man, emaciated and filthy, with a long beard and unkempt hair. He wore shackles on his legs and chains on his wrists, shaking them as he walked. And so the inhabitants of this house spent many dreadful nights lying awake in fear. Illness and eventually death overtook them through lack of sleep and their increasing dread. For even when the ghost was absent, the memory of that horrible apparition preyed on their minds, and their fear itself lasted longer than the initial cause of

that fear. And so eventually the house was deserted and condemned to solitude, left entirely to the ghost. But the house was advertised,[15] in case someone unaware of the evil should wish to buy or rent it.

There came to Athens the philosopher Athenodorus. He read the advertisement, and when he heard the low price, he was suspicious and made some inquiries. He soon learned the whole story and, far from being deterred, was that much more interested in renting the place. When evening began to fall, he requested a bed for himself to be set up in the front of the house, and he asked for some small writing tablets, a stylus, and a lamp. He sent all his servants to the back of the house, and concentrated his mind, eyes, and hand on his writing, lest an unoccupied mind produce foolish fears and cause him to imagine he saw the ghost he had already heard so much about.

At first, as usual, there was only the night silence. Then came the sound of iron clashing, of chains clanking; yet Athenodorus did not raise his eyes or put down his stylus. Instead he concentrated his attention on his work. Then the din grew even louder: and now it was heard at the threshold— now it was inside the room with him! Athenodorus turned, saw, and recognized the ghost. It was standing there, beckoning to him with its finger as if calling to him. Rather than answering the summons, he motioned with his hand that the ghost should wait a while, and he turned back to his writing. The ghost continued rattling its chains right over the philosopher's head. Athenodorus looked around again: sure enough, the ghost was still there, beckoning as before. With no further delay, the philosopher picked up his lamp and followed the phantom. The specter walked very slowly, as if weighed down by the chains. Then it walked to the courtyard of the house and suddenly vanished, abandoning its comrade. Athenodorus, now alone, plucked some grass and leaves to mark the spot where the ghost had disappeared. In the morning he went to the local magistrates and advised that they order the spot to be excavated, which they did. Bones were found, entwined with chains—bones that the body, rotted by time and earth, had left bare and corroded by the chains. These bones were gathered and given a public burial. After these rites had been performed, the house was no longer troubled by spirits.[16] (7.27.5–11)

In keeping with what seems to be a tradition for haunted-house stories, as discussed in Chapter 3, the house itself is described first. Pliny opens by specifying the large size of the house and its bad reputation. It is possible that because the house is described as "large and roomy" (*spatiosa et capax*), and because it is deserted, it would have been on the outskirts of town.[17] Pliny certainly emphasizes the emptiness of the house, with the repetition of words and phrases, as in "And so eventually the house was deserted and condemned to solitude, left entirely to the ghost" (*deserta inde et damnata solitudine domus totaque illi monstro relicta*). The word *desertus* ("deserted," "abandoned") and its forms reappear toward the end of the story: *deserit* applies to the ghost, and lets us know that now the ghost itself, not the inhabitants, is leaving the house. The last *desertus* applies to Athenodorus and indicates that the ghost is indeed gone, even suggesting momentarily that the philosopher might have imagined the apparition. As in Plautus, the house is described as dangerous, though here with the adjectives *infamis* ("disreputable") and *pestilens* ("unhealthy") rather than *scelestus* ("cursed"). *Pestilens,* in fact, was commonly used to describe a house that was unsanitary, as we saw in Cicero's discussion about the moral duty of a realtor (*Off.* 3.13.54). Schwartz theorizes that the combination of the size of the house, its location, its emptiness, and its odd reputation were meant to recall descriptions of Plato's Academy, such as this one found in Cicero: "At the time, the place was empty of crowds . . . when, moreover, we had come to the walks of the Academy, which are deservedly famous, there was that solitude there which we had hoped for" (*Fin.* 5.1.1).[18]

In any case, both Pliny and Cicero make it clear that someone selling a house has a moral duty to disclose information, and that a person would have to be either very ignorant or very foolish to pay full price for a house with the problems described in these scenarios. Both of these ideas are also implied in Tranio's story in the *Mostellaria*. When Tranio says to Theopropides that the murderer of Diapontius was "that man . . . who sold you the house" (480), he seems to be suggesting that Theopropides was cheated—the house where a crime had been committed should have been sold at a discount, but wasn't. Pliny specifies, "the house was advertised, in case someone unaware of the evil should wish to rent or buy it." Plautus's Tranio implies that this was the case with Theopropides—a blow to the old merchant's business sense, in addition to playing off his superstitious nature.

Athenodorus is not superstitious. He is, instead, a rational, reliable witness, someone not prone to fits of imagination. His character adds credibility to the story. Athenodorus is a philosopher, and presumably a well-known one. Pliny brings out this character's importance with the word order, putting his protagonist at the end of a phrase: "There came to Athens the philosopher Athenodorus" (*venit Athenas philosophus Athenodorus*). The identity of this particular character has not been confirmed, but there were at least two known Stoic philosophers of this name. One, surnamed Cordylion, from Tarsus, came to Rome around 70 B.C. at the invitation of Cato and stayed with him. The other, the son of Sandon, was also from Tarsus.[19] He lived in Rome as a teacher and friend of Augustus for many years before returning to his own country, where he died at the age of 82.[20] The two are often confused, and it is not possible to tell which Athenodorus was the protagonist here, or even if he was one of these two at all. Either character would date the story to the first century B.C. or—at the latest—the early first century A.D., nearly one hundred years before Pliny was writing his letters. Schwartz suggests that the presence of a Stoic philosopher in the story strengthens the connection to the Academy.[21] Athenodorus was in any case a familiar figure. In another sense, his exact identity is of little importance—in fact, we should even be suspicious of his name, which might mean "gift of Athens," a name appropriate to the story because Athenodorus rescues Athens from the horror that has been terrorizing it. Athenodorus, who is *not* "unaware of the evil," finds the low rent suspicious and makes inquiries. When he learns the story behind the low rent, and the bad reputation of the house, he is not deterred; in fact, he is all the more intrigued (*immo tanto magis*), adding bravery (or at least scientific curiosity) to his other qualities.

Pliny next focuses on the philosopher's behavior. Athenodorus makes himself comfortable, bringing along his couch, writing instruments, servants, and a lamp. He settles down for the evening with his work, after ordering his servants to retire. Unlike the situation in other haunted-house stories, these servants stay in the house—but farther inside, separated from the protagonist.[22] Because the philosopher is obviously the person to whom the ghost must appear, it does not matter that the servants are in the house. Having the servants present might produce a certain amount of suspense: it adds the possibility that the servants will be frightened by the ghost before Athenodorus can confront it. But, in keeping with tradition, Athenodorus is essentially alone, simply because he is in the room by himself. Pliny specifically describes Athenodorus's precautions against imagining anything; the philosopher knows the story already and does not want to be influenced by it. He focuses on his work so that his imagination will have no chance to wander: "He concentrated his mind, eyes, and hand on his writing, lest an unoccupied mind should cause him to imagine he saw the ghost he had already heard so much about" (*ad scribendum animum oculos manum intendit, ne vacua mens audita . . . simulacra fingeret*). Reason and concentration, it seems, should banish fear.

It has been suggested that Athenodorus's situation has parallels with certain rabbinic texts in which a concentration on reading sacred books wards off the Angel of Death, who cannot strike while someone has the holy words on his lips. For example, the Angel of Death, charged with bringing about the death of Rabbi Nehemiah, found him engrossed in reading the Talmud. But because it was ordained that no one could die while reading the sacred book, the Angel was forced to come up with a stratagem to interrupt Nehemiah's reading.[23] A similar story is told about King David, who was studying the Torah when the Angel of Death came for him.[24] These and other such stories suggest a belief in antiquity that applying oneself to scholarly matters could ward off otherworldly apparitions. The point in the rabbinic examples, however, is that Nehemiah and David are protected not simply because they are concentrating on reading, but because they are reading sacred texts; and though warding off a ghost might be a metaphor for facing death, it is rather different from directly confronting Death personified. It is also interesting to compare modern parapsychological observations on this issue of reading and concentration. When a person is deeply engrossed in reading and writing, events from the external world are excluded, thereby allowing impressions from the unconscious to emerge. In fact, a person may be *more* susceptible to hallucinations than usual.[25]

When Athenodorus begins to hear the noises, which he must recognize as the precursors to the ghost's appearance, he ignores them: "Athenodorus did not raise his eyes or put down his stylus. Instead, he concentrated his attention on his work" (*non tollere oculos, non remittere stilum, sed offirmare animum auribusque praetendere*). Pliny builds suspense in this scene as he did earlier in his more general description of the haunting, by having the sound move closer and closer: "Then the din grew even louder: and now it was heard at the threshold—now it was inside the room" (*crebrescere fragor, adventare et iam ut in limine, iam ut intra limen audiri*). The repetition heightens the effect. Athenodorus's supreme calm is evident from his initial refusal to respond to the beckoning phantom: "Rather than answering the summons, he motioned with his hand that the ghost should wait a while, and he turned back to his writing" (*hic contra ut paulum expectaret manu significat rursusque ceris et stilo incumbit*). At this point the scene becomes rather comic, with the frustrated specter now rattling his chains directly over the head of Athenodorus to get his attention. Pliny may not have intended this scene to be comic, since he introduces the story by saying, "Isn't this story at least as extraordinary and even more horrible [than the previous one]?" (*illud nonne et magis terribile et non minus mirum est*, 7.27.4). Römer argues that the scene is indeed comic, saying that Pliny exaggerates the imperturbability of the philosopher by having the ghost become, for a moment, a comic figure.[26] The problem of interpretation may point to a discrepancy between the author's intent and the effect on the modern reader.

In any case, finally convinced that this is no illusion—and having looked twice to reassure himself (*respicit . . . respicit*)—Athenodorus follows the

ghost into the yard, notes the spot where it vanishes, and informs the au-
thorities about what has happened.[27] It has by this point become clear that
the ghost never intended to harm anyone, but wished only to communicate. It is worth noting that, as in the *Mostellaria,* the ghost appeared in the
presence of a lamp. Athenodorus needs the light to work by, as well as to
be able to see the ghost in the dark, and to follow it; but its presence also
suggests that restless spirits are drawn by the light that is supposed to lead
them to the next world.[28] Unlike in the *Mostellaria,* however, the remains
of this body are exhumed, and a proper burial puts the spirit to rest. To
a certain extent, even this is only implied rather than explicitly stated by
Pliny. When the ghost leads Athenodorus to a particular spot and vanishes,
the philosopher easily deduces that he should dig there to find out what
about this particular location was important to the ghost. When the skeleton entwined in chains is discovered, the next step is also obvious—the
bones must be buried with the proper rituals. Pliny does not spend much
time on this last section of his story: "After these rites had been performed,
the house was no longer troubled by spirits" (*domus postea rite conditis manibus caruit*). He does not describe the burial ritual in any detail at all. His
audience would already have known the ritual, and Pliny, as a storyteller,
was more interested in the ghost and its interaction with the philosopher.
Pliny—and possibly his source as well—put some effort into creating an
air of mystery in this story and building suspense. Once the mystery is un-
covered, the story is essentially over, and it would be anticlimactic to go
into detail at this point. This ending leaves the mystery still largely unexplained, and we are left to wonder whose bones those were and why they
were there.

Pliny's treatment of the ghost itself is particularly interesting. As we have
seen, in most ancient ghost stories there is a specific reason for the haunting
and, more importantly, an identity for the ghost. In Plautus, for example,
Tranio intentionally draws a parallel between Diapontius and Theopropides, both businessmen who must travel overseas. In Pliny's story, the identity of the ghost remains a mystery; although the old man whose ghost
haunts the place was buried on the premises, the reason for his being there
is never stated, but rather is left to our imagination. Was he, like the fictional Diapontius, a murder victim? The chains add another element to the
mystery: Was the man imprisoned for a crime, and if so, why was he then
buried here? Why was he *buried* with the chains and not found chained *to*
something, such as a wall? The ghost's long hair and beard, and ragged
clothes, suggest a lengthy imprisonment.

In general, Pliny concentrates on the sounds caused by the ghost rather than on the ghost's physical appearance, but he describes the ghost at the beginning of the story: "There appeared a phantom, an old man, emaciated and filthy, with a long beard and unkempt hair. He wore shackles on his legs and chains on his wrists" (*apparebat idolon, senex macie et squalore confectus, promissa barba, horrenti capillo: cruribus compedes, manibus catenas gerebat*). This initial physical description of the ghost is tightly packed, with much asyndeton. Pliny's descriptions of men often focus on hair. Compare, for example, Pliny's *senex* here with his illustration of the philosopher Euphrates in letter 1.10.7: "[He had] long hair, and a huge grey beard" (*demissus capillus, ingens et cana barba*). Considering the connections with period portraiture, the description of the old man in 7.27 is a good example of late Hellenistic realism.[29] In fact, the ghost looks like a philosopher, resembling not only Pliny's description of Euphrates, but descriptions of philosophers in general, suggesting again the possible connection between the haunted house and the Academy.[30] There is certainly nothing corresponding to the ghost of the old man in any of the other ancient ghost stories. As noted earlier, however, there may be a more practical explanation for the ghost's long hair and beard: he was imprisoned and presumably not visiting a barber regularly.

Once Pliny describes the ghost's physical appearance, he does not return to it again. For the rest of the story, Pliny describes the ghost in only two ways, neither of which refers to any of the physical attributes mentioned in that initial sentence. First, he uses a large number of single words that mean "ghost" or "apparition": the ghost is variously *idolon, imago, monstrum, simulacrum* or *effigies*.[31] At the end of the story he uses the general word for spirits of the dead: *manes*. Second, Pliny describes the ghost's actions: it "was standing there, beckoning with its finger" (*stabat innuebatque digito*), it "walked very slowly" (*ibat lento gradu*). But the phantom's principal action is its constant chain-rattling, which fills the story with sound effects.

In fact, the haunted-house story in Pliny's letter concentrates not on the physical characteristics of the ghost but on the sounds that signal its imminent arrival and then its materialization. In this particular story, the sound effects relate to the consequent mental state of the inhabitants: their terror arises largely in anticipation of the ghost's arrival rather than from its actual presence. The treatment of how the ghost haunts the inhabitants is very specific—more detailed than in other cases from antiquity—and is drawn out to create suspense. The sound of the chains is the first thing Pliny mentions about the ghost, and from there he places emphasis on the sequence of events and on the ominous atmosphere created by the effect of the sound moving closer and closer to the terrified inhabitants, using a sequence of adverbs to create the suspense: *primo, deinde, mox, inde, nam interdiu quoque.* The noise is heard before the image is seen, emphasizing the terror produced by the sound that precedes the ghost. The sound conditions the inhabitants: they know from experience that after the noise, the horrible apparition will appear, and this knowledge works on their mental state to such an extent that they do not even need to see the ghost to get sick—and even die—from terror: they spend "dreadful nights lying awake in fear" (*dirae noctes per metum vigilabantur*). Why they did not just leave immediately is a question people have been asking about the residents of haunted houses for ages. Tranio's explanation that Philolaches left because the house was haunted makes the *Mostellaria* one of the few stories in which the inhabitants were supposedly so sensible.[32] In Pliny, the inhabitants sicken and then die from the effect: "Even when the ghost was absent, the memory of the apparition preyed on their minds, and their fear itself lasted longer than the initial cause of that fear" (*quamquam abscesserat imago, memoria imaginis oculis inerrabat, longiorque causis timoris timor erat*). Fear, amplified by imagination, causes their deaths. This ghost continues to trouble people even when he is not there, as the disturbing vision stays with them.

This situation does not occur in any other ancient ghost story, though the vivid effect of memory on the imagination in general is reflected in Cicero's description of a stroll around the Academy: "Plato came to my mind, whom we accept as the first who was accustomed to hold discussions here; and indeed, the nearby gardens not only brought the memory to me, but seemed to put the vision of Plato himself before my eyes."[33] Pliny's concentration on sound is actually far more effective than repeated descriptions of the ghost would be, since imagination can conjure up phantoms at least as terrifying as reality. Repeated descriptions of a thin, old ghost might make him seem more mundane and less shocking. So the focus on sound rather than sight leaves it up to Pliny's audience to imagine its own terrifying apparition. Pliny emphasizes the emotional state of the inhabitants with repetition of words for fear, such as *formido, timor,* and *metus. Inanes metus,* "foolish fears," in 7.27.7 also echoes Pliny's remark at 7.27.1, when he asks whether apparitions are "unreal images that take their forms from our own anxieties" (*an inania et vana ex metu nostro imaginem accipere*). Such fears help explain why Athenodorus wants to occupy his mind during his vigil: he is aware of the tricks the imagination can play and hopes to guard against them.

After this explanation of the effect of the ghost, Pliny continues to describe sounds caused by the ghost rather than its physical characteristics.

Placing great emphasis on the chains, he mentions them more frequently than anything else in the story: "the sound of metal" (*sonus ferri*); "the clanking of chains" (*strepitus vinculorum*); "shackles on his legs, chains on his wrists" (*cruribus compedes, manibus catenas*); "iron clashing, chains clanking" (*concuti ferrum, vincula moveri*); "it kept rattling the chains" (*catenis insonabat*); "weighed down by chains" (*gravis vinculis*); "bones entwined with chains" (*ossa inserta catenis*); "corroded by the chains" (*exesa vinculis*). Such repetitions suggest the influence of an oral tradition. But the chains also serve an important purpose in the narrative: they, along with the bones, turn out to be real, physical evidence of the haunting. They corroborate Athenodorus's story, because he knew exactly where to dig to find these material remnants. They also deepen the mystery, leaving many unanswered questions: Why was the old man in chains? Was he rattling them not only to draw attention to himself, but to point out the extent of his torment? And how long had the bones been buried there? Long enough not only for the flesh to have rotted away, but also for the iron to have done some damage to them (many months, possibly many years). The existence of the chains leaves a lot for the reader to fill in with his imagination. Could this man have been a houseguest, robbed, imprisoned, murdered, and hidden? Or could he have been a criminal, and if so, why was justice not sought through the proper channels? Pliny himself does not look for an explanation. This ghost does not speak and tell its story; it only gestures and rattles chains.[34] Ghosts bearing chains do not appear elsewhere in the surviving literature from Greece or Rome, but in Pliny's story, they seem too ingrained an element for him to have invented them. There may be a connection between this chain-rattling, house-bound ghost and the belief that iron can bind spirits and keep them restrained to certain locations.[35] More important, just as the memory of the ghostly apparition affected the imagination of the house's residents, so, too, the unexplained mystery of the ghost's origins works on our own minds, proving again that what can be imagined may be more powerful than what is explicitly described.

The Apparitions of Nero and Drusus

Although Pliny nowhere else describes a haunting in so much detail, a small episode from another of his letters provides a point of comparison to the apparition in the haunted house of 7.27. In Pliny 5.5 we have an account of a vision that is in several respects quite similar to the discussion of *phantasmata* in 7.27; yet, somewhat surprisingly, in 5.5 Pliny does not bring up

the subject of apparitions. Here Pliny expresses regret at the news of Gaius
Fannius's death, and says that what bothers him the most is that Fannius left
his work unfinished—he was writing a history of the crimes of Nero's
reign. But Fannius had had a presentiment that he would die with the work
unfinished (5.5.5–7):

> Indeed, Gaius Fannius foresaw what would happen to him long before
> it actually did. During the silence of the night he dreamed that he was
> lying quietly on his bed the way he always worked—he had before him his
> writing-case (as was his habit). Soon he imagined that Nero came to him,
> sat down next to him on the bed, picked up the first book that Fannius
> had published about Nero's crimes, read it over, did the same thing with
> the second and third books, and then left. Fannius was terrified and inter-
> preted this to mean that he would finish writing just as much as Nero had
> read—and so it was.[36]

Pliny apparently does not consider Nero to be a ghost; he uses none of the
words for "apparition" that we have seen in his other ghost stories. Rather,
he specifies that the apparition is a presentiment, an omen of things to
come, a vision to be interpreted. Pliny also makes it clear that Nero, omen
or not, is the product of Fannius's imagination. The event is removed from
reality: Fannius was lying in bed dreaming (*visus est*), and within the dream
he saw Nero (*imaginatus est*). Nevertheless, the similarities between this
scene and the story of the apparition of 7.27.5–11 are striking, with parallels in situation, narrative structure, and literary phrasing. The phrase "during the silence of the night" occurs in both stories (*per nocturnam quietem,*
5.5.5; *per silentium noctis,* 7.27.5) and establishes more generally that such
visions, whether omens or hauntings, are more likely to occur in the quiet
night hours.[37] Also similar is the narrative sequence "soon he imagined"
(*mox imaginatus est*), which parallels "soon there appeared" (*mox apparebat,*
7.27.5): when someone is sitting quietly at night minding his own business,
something unusual happens. And although Pliny makes clear that Fannius
imagined what he saw, we should not ignore the relationship between the
phrase "he imagined" (*imaginatus est*) and the word *imago,* which Pliny uses
twice to describe the apparition of the old man.

   Another similarity is the occupation of the person to whom the vision
appears. Like Athenodorus, Fannius is calmly absorbed in his writing. Unlike Athenodorus, however, Fannius is not expecting to see anything. But
Fannius was probably working on the continuation of his history of Nero's

reign, and so had on his mind the tyrant whom he evidently despised and feared. That he should imagine he saw Nero, then, is not so very strange. Moreover, the presentiment is of the sort that can easily be self-fulfilling: Fannius may have psychologically convinced himself that it was bound to come true. It is even possible that Pliny intended a pun on the word *compositus:* while it often means "settled in place," it can also mean "laid out on one's deathbed."[38] Fannius interpreted the vision to mean that he would live long enough to finish writing only as much as Nero had read—the first three books, the only ones already written—and that is exactly what happened.

Pliny describes a similar experience in letter 3.5, in which his uncle, Pliny the Elder, is visited by the ghost of Drusus Nero,[39] who encourages him to write a history of the German Wars (3.5.4):

> [Among his works were] *Twenty Books on the Wars in Germany,* in which he wrote about all the wars that we had waged with the Germans. He began when he was a soldier in Germany, having been advised to do so by a dream: the phantom of Drusus Nero, who had extended his victory far into Germany and died there, stood by him as he was sleeping and entrusted him with his memory and entreated him not to let his memory suffer the injury of oblivion.[40]

In this letter Pliny uses words and phrases similar to those in 1.18, 5.5, and 7.27, such as *ei quiescenti* and *effigies*. In this case, too, we have an apparition connected with writing; but the effect of the dream is the opposite of what we see in 7.27 and 5.5. In 7.27, Athenodorus ceased writing at the ghost's request, and in 5.5 Fannius was so affected by his nightmare that he never finished writing his history.[41] In 3.5, however, the apparition inspired the elder Pliny to write a long history. Since Drusus Nero was a far more benign figure than the emperor Nero, the inspiration is understandable.

In his several letters describing supernatural events, the younger Pliny draws no explicit distinctions between ghosts, warning apparitions, and dream-visions, and does not explain why some of them may be interpreted as omens while others may not. He also makes no distinctions in his use of vocabulary to describe such events, applying terms such as *effigies* to both the ghost of the old man and the figure of Drusus Nero who appeared to the elder Pliny in a dream. Pliny's widely varying interpretations of such events also suggest that he did not hold any particularly religious beliefs about an afterlife. Ultimately, Pliny is hesitant even to express an opinion about whether *phantasmata* exist. Although he seems convinced by the stories told by his servants, he concludes his letter to Sura without committing to either side of the issue. He urges Sura, however, not to be so indecisive: "While you may argue for either side, as you usually do, yet try to come down more strongly on one or the other, so as not to leave me in suspense and uncertainty, since the point is that I am consulting you to end my doubts" (7.27.16).[42] Unfortunately, we do not have Sura's reply to this letter.

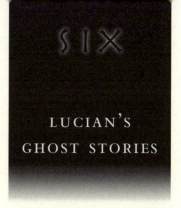

SIX

LUCIAN'S
GHOST STORIES

TWO WELL-KNOWN GHOST STORIES SURVIVE IN THE WORKS OF THE satirist Lucian (fl. A.D. 160–180), both of them in his dialogue *Philopseudes* ("The Lover of Lies"), in which he satirizes superstition.[1] In this dialogue, Lucian's spokesman, the rational Tychiades, begins a conversation with his friend Philocles about why men love to tell lies and outrageous stories. "Can you tell me, Philocles, why it is that many people are so fond of telling lies that they enjoy saying things that are unsound and pay particular attention to those who tell those sorts of stories?"[2] Tychiades criticizes intelligent men who are nevertheless lovers of lies (φιλοψευδεῖς, *philopseudeis*), and cites Homer and Herodotus as two of his main examples, finding it ridiculous, for one thing, that the god Pan came from Arcadia to participate in the battle of Marathon.[3]

Explaining to Philocles why the subject is on his mind, Tychiades tells him about a recent visit to the house of Eucrates, an invalid recovering from an unspecified foot disease. He had found Eucrates in the company of the doctor Antigonos and three philosophers: the Peripatetic Cleodemos, the Stoic Deinomachos, and the Platonist Ion. Lucian sets the theme by having Tychiades interrupt the company during a discussion about healing amulets. His mockery of their superstitious beliefs challenges Eucrates and the others to try to persuade Tychiades to believe in the supernatural. The sequence of stories they proceed to tell forms the basis for this dialogue, as Lucian links one tale to another until most of the well-known superstitions of his day have been exposed.[4]

The first story, concerning a man bitten on the foot by a snake, follows naturally from Eucrates' illness.[5] The subsequent stories include tales of walking statues, visions of the underworld, and ghosts. We have already seen several of these stories in Chapter 2, such as the ones about the little bronze figurine of Hippocrates and the giant apparition of Hekate, who opens a chasm to the underworld (*Philops*. 21–22). Though Lucian criticizes many superstitions, largely through hyperbole, perhaps his most effective exaggerations come in the treatment of the two ghost stories. The first, told by Eucrates himself, concerns a visit paid to him by his dead wife (*Philops.* 27). The second, about a haunted house at Corinth, is told by the Pythagorean philosopher Arignotos (*Philops.* 30–31). Arignotos also provides the link to the last and most well-known story, that of the Sorcerer's Apprentice: although this story is told by Eucrates, the Sorcerer turns out to be Arignotos's teacher, the Egyptian Pancrates.[6]

Is There Wife after Death?

At *Philopseudes* 27, Eucrates tells how the ghost of his wife suddenly appeared one day, returning from the dead because her sandal was not burned with the rest of her belongings and consequently her spirit could not rest:

> Eucrates, as if reminded [of the story] at the sight of his sons, said, "So may my sons here prosper"—taking them by the hand—"I will tell you the truth, Tychiades. Everyone knows how I loved my dear departed wife, the mother of these children. I showed my devotion in everything I did for her, not only while she was alive, but even when she died, burning all her jewelry together with the clothes she had liked when she was alive. On the seventh day after she died, I was lying here on this couch, just as I am now, consoling myself; for I was quietly reading Plato's little book on the nature of the soul. While I was thus engaged, Demainete herself came in and sat down nearby, about where Eucratides is now," he said, pointing out the younger of his sons. And the boy immediately shuddered childishly, having already turned pale at the story. Eucrates continued, "I embraced her, and weeping, wailed aloud. But she did not allow me to cry, and instead rebuked me because, although I had freely given everything else to her, I had neglected to burn one of her gilt sandals with the other. It had fallen under the wooden chest, and because of this we did not find it, and had burned only the one. We were still talking when that damned little dog, the Maltese one, barked from under the couch, and she vanished at his bark. But I did indeed find the sandal under the chest, and burned it later."[7]

Some commentators have asserted that this story is clearly modeled on the account of Melissa and Periander in Herodotus 5.92.η.[8] The Corinthian tyrant Periander had misplaced something entrusted to him by a friend, and decided to consult the spirit of his dead wife (whom he himself had killed), to ask where he had put it. He sent a messenger to the Oracle of the Dead on the river Acheron in Thesprotia. When Melissa's ghost was conjured up, she refused to answer Periander's question, saying that she was cold and naked because he had cremated her without her clothes, after "putting his loaves into a cold oven" (ἐπὶ ψυχρὸν τὸν ἰπνὸν Περίανδρον τοὺς ἄρτους ἐπέβαλε, 5.92.η)—that is, having had sexual relations with her dead body. When this message was reported to him, Periander commanded all the women of Corinth to strip and give him their clothes to burn. Melissa's ghost was appeased and answered his inquiry. This story of Periander's shameless excesses occurs at the end of Socles' speech on the evils of tyranny to explain why the Corinthians will not help the tyrant Hippias return to Athens. One commentator calls Lucian's story of Eucrates and his wife "a travesty of Periander's rites for Melissa," saying that Lucian has merely adapted the story of Melissa to a more trivial setting. That is, where Periander has to burn the clothes of every woman in Corinth, Eucrates has only to burn his wife's slipper to appease her ghost.[9] From Lucian's reference to Herodotus earlier in this dialogue, it is clear that he had the historian in mind. But Lucian has not simply adapted Herodotus. There are several important differences in the way each story is told.

For one thing, there is a major difference in the manner of each ghost's visitation. Periander had intentionally consulted Melissa's ghost, a case of necromancy. Periander was not even present when his wife's shade was summoned, and instead heard everything from the messenger. In Lucian's story, however, the dead wife Demainete comes to visit Eucrates of her own accord, a case of haunting. And there is a good amount of personal interaction between the husband and wife. Demainete is an unusually solid ghost: Eucrates can grasp her and catch her in his arms. This does not happen in other cases where people are visited by the ghosts of close friends or spouses. When Achilles tries to grasp the dream-ghost of Patroclus, for example, he clasps only thin air (*Il.* 23.99–101). Similarly, Aeneas cannot embrace Creusa's ghost (*Aen.* 2.792–94). Demainete is evidently a sort of embodied ghost, though not a true revenant, and she is referred to only by name and by pronouns in the story, and never by any of the words for "ghost." Yet her body had been burned on the pyre, and at the end of the story she simply vanishes into thin air. Her solidity in the story comes across as mundane, if not actually ridiculous. Meanwhile, Lucian, through Eucrates, does not otherwise bother to describe Demainete, failing to mention, for example, whether she is wearing all of her clothes except for the offending sandal. More importantly Herodotus's story is itself an exaggeration: Periander's burning of the clothes of every woman in Corinth illustrates the excesses of a tyrant, as he grossly overcompensates for Melissa's complaint about her clothing. The episode in Herodotus is *already* a travesty of proper funeral rites. There is no indication that Melissa intended to haunt Periander either for her murder or for the improper funeral (not to mention the necrophilia). The emphasis falls instead on Periander and his tyranny.

Another major difference in the two stories is Lucian's inclusion of apparently trivial details for satiric effect. Lucian describes a specifically domestic scene, where Eucrates is reading a book—not coincidentally, Plato on the nature of the soul (the *Phaedo*). His dead wife walks into the room and sits down. Rather than lamenting her pitiable state of limbo, as Melissa does by describing herself as cold and naked, Demainete rebukes her husband (ᾐτιᾶτο).[10] As Eucrates recounts this scene, his young son, sitting nearby, grows pale and shudders at the recollection of his dead mother's visit, which adds an element of melodrama. The neglected sandal itself seems trivial in comparison with Melissa's complete lack of clothing, and particularly trivial is the location of the sandal behind a chest. But Lucian is most likely satirizing yet another aspect of religious superstition. Monosandalism, which is attributed to gods, heroes, and particularly persons engaged in rituals, belongs to the realm of religion or magic, and is sometimes associated with binding spells (or unbinding spells).[11] It represents a liminal status, having one foot in this material world and one foot in the spirit world. Lucian has satirized yet another folk-belief by losing it behind the furniture, considering monosandalism as ineffectual for spiritual enlightenment as amulets are for medicine.

Also deceptively trivial is the role of the barking dog. On this detail, Anderson comments, "[Demainete's] ghost is driven away not at dawn or cockcrow, but by the yelping of a pet Maltese," and he describes the incident as yet another indignity added by Lucian to satirize Herodotus's story. While Lucian may have intended the dog's interference as a trivializing "indignity" we should remember that the role of the dog follows the folklore tradition of animal sensitivity to the supernatural. Lucian's satiric intent probably lies not so much in the inclusion of a dog barking but in bothering to specify the *type* of dog. The Maltese, a popular pet both then and now, is a miniature breed with long white fur.[12] Lucian plays on folklore tradition by having a tiny, pampered, annoying dog upset the action rather than the large, noble shepherding or hunting dogs usually found in such scenes— such as Eumaios's dogs recognizing the presence of the disguised Athena (*Od.* 16.155–63).[13]

In sum, despite the similarities between the ghost-wife stories of Herodotus and Lucian, we need to stress the fact that similarity in the stories does not necessarily imply derivation. Lucian's story may allude to that of Herodotus, but it has little in common with that earlier story. There are more dissimilarities than similarities between the two, and Lucian's cannot be said to be a direct adaptation of Herodotus's version, despite his probable familiarity with it. These stories are more likely relatively independent variations on a more general theme, that of ghosts requesting proper burial, with each author adapting that theme for a particular purpose: Herodotus to illustrate a tyrant's excess, and Lucian to satirize the trendy fascination with magic and superstition in his time.

Is There a Philosopher in the House?

In Lucian's second ghost story, which concerns a haunted house in Corinth, the consensus is that Lucian was borrowing from literature again—in this case, from letter 7.27 of Pliny the Younger. Anderson says, "Detailed comparison with Pliny's wholly serious version . . . shows how little Lucian has been able to add; but such a theme is *de rigueur* in any account of *deisidaimonia:* we should not necessarily assume that Lucian held as closely to an 'original' in each of the other tales." [14] Jones, too, believes that Lucian must have been adapting Pliny: "Arignotos' tale of the ghost that he laid in a house at Corinth resembles down to small details one told by the Younger Pliny about a philosopher at Athens." [15] But Anderson and Jones cite no evidence other than this story and Lucian's erudition in general to show that Lucian was familiar with Pliny's writings, and Radermacher attributes both Pliny's and Lucian's stories to an oral tradition. [16]

After Eucrates finishes the story of Demainete's visit, Arignotus the Pythagorean philosopher arrives and asks what the group was talking about. Pointing at Tychiades, Eucrates says, "We have been trying to persuade this stubborn man that ghosts exist, and that the spirits of the dead walk above the ground and appear to whomever they wish." [17] Arignotus suggests that perhaps Tychiades was willing to believe that only the spirits of those who had died by violence walk the earth. "No," says another, "he thinks that such things do not exist at all." [18] Joining the group's attempt to persuade Tychiades, Arignotos tells the story of one of his own encounters with the supernatural, a tale that is indeed reminiscent of Pliny's haunted-house story:

> "Well," he said, "if you ever go to Corinth, ask where the house of Eubatides is, and when it is pointed out to you beside the Cornel Grove, go there and tell the door-keeper Tibeios that you wish to see where the Pythagorean Arignotos bested the daimon and made the house habitable from then on."

"What's the story, Arignotos?" asked Eucrates. "The house was unin-habitable for a long time," he replied, "because of terrifying phenomena, and any person who tried to live there soon fled, panic-stricken, pursued by some fearful and menacing phantom. So the house was starting to col-lapse, and the roof was falling in, and in short there was no one brave enough to enter it.

"When I heard this, I gathered up my books—for I have quite a few Egyptian books about this very subject—and went to the house at the hour when people usually go to sleep. My host tried to turn me back, and all but physically restrained me when he learned where I was going—to face a known evil, he thought. I went in alone, taking a lamp, and put the lamp down in the largest room. Sitting on the ground, I was reading peacefully, when the daimon appeared, thinking he was approaching just any man, and hoping to frighten me just as he had the others. He was filthy and long-haired and blacker than darkness itself. Standing over me, he made an attempt on me, attacking from all sides to see if he could con-quer me, changing himself now into a dog, now into a bull or lion. But I had ready the most horrible Egyptian curse, and speaking in the Egyptian tongue I drove him away and bound him in a corner of a dark room. Observing where he sank down, I rested for what was left of the night.

"Early in the morning, when everyone had given up hope and expected to find me a corpse like the others, I came out entirely unexpectedly, and went to Eubatides with the good news that he could live once more in the house, which was now purified and freed from fear. Then, taking him and many others—they followed along because the incident was so marvel-ous—I led them to the place where I had seen the daimon sink into the earth, and I urged them to dig there with hoes and shovels. Doing this, they found, buried at nearly six feet down, a rotting corpse, with only the bones remaining in order. After we dug it up and buried it, the house from then on ceased to be troubled by phantoms." [19]

The following chart illustrates the parallels between the narrative sequence of this story and Pliny's, along with some differences in the details: [20]

PLINY 7.27.5–11	LUCIAN *Philopseudes* 30–31
The story is told in the third person, by an unidentified narrator (not necessarily Pliny).	The story is told in the first person, by the protagonist himself.
The setting is a house in Athens, not specified.	The setting is a house in Corinth, specified as belonging to Eubatides, being next to the Kraneion, and having Tibeus as porter.

The protagonist is the philosopher Athenodorus.

The protagonist is the philosopher Arignotus.

The phenomena described include the apparition of an old man in rattling chains, with the effects of insomnia, illness, and death on the inhabitants.

The phenomena described include a fearful specter, which chases and ultimately kills the inhabitants.

The house is up for sale, and Athenodorus rents it.

Arignotus, although his host tries to dissuade him, wants to see the house.

Athenodorus goes with his servants, whom he orders to sleep in the interior of the house.

Arignotus goes alone, armed with books on Egyptian magic.

He settles down to his writing.

He settles down to his reading.

The rumored phantom appears, and invites him to follow it.

The daimon appears, black as the shadows, and tries to conquer him first as a dog, then as a bull, then as a lion.

He follows it, finally, and the phantom disappears in a spot in the yard.

With incantations and Egyptian spells, he restricts the ghost to a corner of the room, where it sinks into the ground.

There is an excavation of the spot: they find the bones, and after a public funeral, the hauntings cease.

He goes to say that the house is freed; they dig, find bones, and bury them; in the future the hauntings do not occur again.

Although there are some differences in the stories, the essential plot archetype remains.[21] The two main differences in the stories are the personalities of the philosophers and the presentations of the ghosts. Lucian relies on the exaggerated character of Arignotos to show how ridiculous and unreliable the story is. The dialogue form allows Arignotos, narrating in the first person, to focus on himself and his behavior, as opposed to Pliny's third-person narrative, which focuses on the ghost.

Lucian introduces Arignotos into the dialogue by having Tychiades assume that this new arrival will force some sense into the group that has been telling such outrageous supernatural stories: "And I, when I saw him, breathed a sigh of relief, thinking that the man had come like an axe to fell the lies. 'This wise man will shut them up when they tell such monstrous stories,' I said to myself." [22] Tychiades soon realizes he is mistaken, however, as Arignotos turns out to be the worst liar of them all, launching into a self-centered story about his own courage and how he was the only person who could rid the haunted house of its ghost. He begins his story by saying that if Tychiades should go to Corinth, he should ask to see the place where Arignotos drove away the daimon. No one, he says, had the courage to enter the house and face the ghost. Arignotos insists on staying in the house even though the owner tries to talk him out of it. He enters the house alone, unlike Athenodorus, who had servants with him. As in Pliny, we find an emphasis on study: in this case, Arignotos is armed with his books on Egyptian magic. With mock humility, he sits on the ground to read them. The poor ghost, he continues, had no idea what it was up against, thinking it was approaching an ordinary man and hoping to frighten Arignotos as it had the others who came to the house.

In other words, Arignotos is an exaggeration of the type of protagonist associated with ghost stories, such as the quiet and logical Athenodorus or the poet Simonides, rewarded for his sense by a grateful dead man (Cic. *Div.* 1.27). Athenodorus was merely suspicious of the low rent and curious about the rumors concerning the house, and he remained a very low-key figure while the storyteller focused attention on the ghost. Arignotos, on the other hand, seeing himself as a hero, makes it clear that he went to the house with the intention of ridding it of the ghost. In this respect he more closely resembles Euthymus, who fought the ghost of Temesa (Paus. 6.6.7–11). Arignotos, however, is openly scornful of others for their fears and boastful about his wide knowledge of Egyptian magic, with which he conquers the terrible phantom. Apparently Arignotos's epic struggle with the ghost covered several rooms in the house: at first he was sitting and reading in the largest room, but he conquers the ghost in another room, a dark one—evidently not the room the lamp was in. He adds that he rested, undisturbed, until morning. As Anderson says, Arignotos turns out to be a *magus gloriosus* when describing his "battle" with the ghost. [23]

As with the treatment of the philosopher, Lucian's treatment of the ghost consists largely of hyperbole, presenting us with a kind of ghost that is relatively rare in the extant classical literature. Nardi remarks that the elderly ghost in Pliny's story, in keeping with Pliny's original question about whether phantasms keep their own forms, preserves the appearance of the dead man. [24] The ghost in Lucian's story does not have any specific appearance apart from its transformations, although it is described as "filthy and long-haired and blacker than darkness" (αὐχμηρὸς καὶ κομήτης καὶ μελάντερος τοῦ ζόφου). What this person looked like in life is left ambiguous, and the ghost comes across as less human than most, fitting the conception of the "evil daimon" held by the ancients in a general sense. Its long hair, as in Pliny's version, provides additional support for Schwartz's suggestion that the ghosts of these haunted houses may have a connection with philosophers. Arignotos himself is twice described by Tychiades as having long hair (κομήτης, *Philops*. 29; κόμην, *Philops*. 32). The word αὐχμηρός (*auchmēros*), however, may have a particular association with ghosts. In Euripides' *Orestes,* for example, Menelaus is upset by Orestes' disheveled appearance, saying he looks like something from the underworld: "I saw one of the dead . . . savage-looking, with filthy locks" (τίνα δέδορκα νερτέρων . . . ὡς ἠγρίωσαι πλόκαμον αὐχμηρόν, 385–87).

Moreover, this long-haired ghost is not simply black. In a nice example of hyperbole, Arignotos says the ghost is "blacker than darkness" (μελάντερος τοῦ ζόφου). Whereas the ghost in Pliny's story unintentionally frightens people in its attempt to attract attention, Lucian's ghost actively chases people away from the house. Like the fictional Diapontius of Plautus's *Mostellaria,* this ghost apparently wants to retain possession of its house and be left alone. Unlike Diapontius, this ghost does not try to say so. This house, like the one Pliny describes, is deserted; Lucian adds that it is in disrepair, with its roof falling in. As in Pliny's story, the ghost here appears in the presence of a lamp—in fact, Arignotos places some emphasis on this fact, mentioning the lamp not once but twice: "I took a lamp . . . I put down the lamp" (ἐγὼ δὲ λύχνον λαβὼν . . . καταθεὶς τὸ φῶς). On the one hand, he needs the light to read by; on the other hand, the contrast between light and darkness reflects the difference between the land of the living and the land of the dead and the idea that restless spirits are drawn to the light.[25] In this story, no noise precedes the appearance of the ghost. Rather, the ghost appears suddenly, adding to Arignotos's reputation for courage as the ghost fails to catch him unprepared.

Anderson observes that Lucian's main addition to the story is "the ghost's irrelevant display of changing its shape,"[26] as the ghost transforms itself first into a dog, then a bull, then a lion. But the changes are hardly irrelevant. Unlike many ghosts, this one is aggressive and attacks, and has more in common with the "embodied ghosts" or revenants such as the Hero of Temesa (Paus. 6.6.7–11).[27] In Anderson's view, these transformations do nothing for the story. But surely they are yet another instance of hyperbole, adding to Arignotos's stature as a *magus gloriosus,* as these menacing beasts—and the fact that the ghost has this shape-shifting power—do not alarm him in the least. This aligns him with epic heroes of mythology, such as Peleus and Menelaus. Peleus struggled to hold the shape-shifting Thetis in order to win her hand in marriage: she became, successively, fire, water, a lioness, and a tree.[28] Menelaus, stranded after the Trojan War, finds

out how to get home to Sparta by wrestling the sea-god Proteus, who
changes into a lion, a snake, a leopard, and a boar, among other things.[29]

In Lucian's context, the shape-shifting ability of this ghost may help
further identify it as an evil daimon rather than the ghost of an individual. Another shape-shifting evil daimon appears in the works of a slightly
later author, Flavius Philostratus, in his *Life of Apollonius of Tyana* 4.10.
Apollonius was a philosopher interested in mysticism, much like Arignotos.
Philostratus tells how Apollonius went to cure a plague at Ephesus. Seeing
an old beggar in the theater near the image of the Avenging God (Hercules),
he instructed people to stone the beggar. Reluctant at first, the people began to stone the old man, who at first had seemed blind, but who now
glared at them with eyes full of fire, at which the Ephesians recognized that
the old beggar man was actually a daimon. They continued to stone him
until he was buried beneath a pile of rocks. When they removed the stones,
they found that the beggar had disappeared, and in his place there was "a
dog, which very much resembled a Molossian dog,[30] but was the size of a
very large lion" (κύων δὲ τὸ μὲν εἶδος ὅμοιος τῷ ἐκ Μολοττῶν, μέ-
γεθος δὲ κατὰ τὸν μέγιστον λέοντα). The statue of the Avenging God
was then set up over the spot where the apparition (φάσμα) was killed.
The philosopher Apollonius is similar to Arignotos, and there is the possibility that Philostratus knew Lucian's *Philopseudes* and borrowed the shape-
shifting daimon from him; but shape-shifting was a common demonic
talent.[31]

Moreover, this is not the first time in the dialogue that Lucian refers to
shape-shifting and to the connection between certain animals and magic.
At *Philopseudes* 14, Cleodemus tells the story of a Hyperborean magician
who drew down the moon, which changed shape several times: "At first
she exhibited the shape of a woman; then she became a beautiful cow; then
she appeared to be a puppy" (τὸ μὲν γὰρ πρῶτον γυναικείαν μορφὴν
ἐπεδείκνυτο, εἶτα βοῦς ἐγίγνετο πάγκαλος, εἶτα σκύλαξ ἐφαίνετο).
In addition to the puppy mentioned here, a small dog appears in the story
of Eucrates' wife given above, and fierce dogs "larger than Indian elephants" accompany the apparition of Hekate in the story Eucrates tells at
Philopseudes 22–24. He describes those dogs as "black . . . and shaggy, with
filthy tangled hair" (μέλανες . . . καὶ λάσιοι πιναρᾷ καὶ αὐχμώσῃ τῇ
λάχνῃ, *Philops.* 24). The ghost confronted by Arignotos fits this description
even before turning into a dog. Lions, too, are mentioned frequently in the
dialogue, particularly toward the beginning in the discussion of curative
amulets: various parts of the lion, such as its skin, paws, and whiskers, are
useful in certain remedies (*Philops.* 7).

Although animal imagery occurs frequently in ghost stories from around the world, there is little evidence that animal ghosts are connected to a belief in metempsychosis.[32] The order of progressive shape-changing in Lucian's story and others probably has nothing to do with that. But the shape originally taken voluntarily by the ghost may say something about its temperament. If it takes a gentle form, such as that of a bird or rabbit, no one need worry. But a ghost that takes a more ferocious form, such as that of a bull, intends to terrify people, and it is worthwhile to find someone who can confront the ghost—as Arignotos does here. In the folklore of many countries, the bird is the most common shape taken by those ghosts who do take animal shape; and the bird is, moreover, the best known of all soul-images, even in antiquity.[33] The form of a bull (or cow or ox) is less common, and tends to be adopted only by particularly violent spirits.[34] The ghost Arignotos describes, which at one point takes the form of a bull, is quite violent. But another popular guise for ghosts to assume is that of a dog. According to the Greeks and Romans, it was not unusual for *daimones* to appear as vicious dogs.[35]

After Arignotos subdues the ghost, he spends a peaceful night, and in the morning informs the owner that the house is purged. Like Athenodorus, Arignotos leads people to the spot where the ghost disappeared. They dig down six feet and discover bones. There are no chains to be found here; in fact, there is very little mystery at all, as Arignotos has focused the story on himself rather than on the generic, depersonalized ghost, malevolent though it is. We do not wonder how or why the bones were buried in this house; we do not care who this person was, or whether the spirit finds peace. Whereas the ghost in Pliny's story ultimately comes across as sympathetic, Lucian's ghost is not sympathetic in the least. As Finucane observes, "In the Athenian example, the ghost beckons the philosopher to follow it, but in the Corinthian it is coerced into the ground. Charity toward the dead has become combat with evil."[36] This does not necessarily imply any sort of chronological progression in the stories. The evil daimon conquered by Arignotos behaves much the same as that in Pausanias's story of the Hero of Temesa, which has to be appeased with its own shrine; "charity toward the dead" is also practiced by Simonides in Cicero's story of the grateful dead man, among others.

Unlike Pliny, who creates a psychological atmosphere for his story and wonders whether ghosts might be real, Lucian intentionally satirizes the irrational beliefs of gullible people who try to convince rational people like Tychiades that there are such things as ghosts. Pliny is a possible target of Lucian's satire; philosophers from many schools are definite targets. Lucian satirizes the religious beliefs underlying such stories, and includes the Egyptian spells and other types of magic that had come into such vogue. The

Pythagoreans "were indeed often necromancers, convinced defenders of spiritualism, in which . . . they sought an immediate proof of the immortality of the soul, and by their doctrines they contributed to keeping alive the superstitious fear attached to omission of burial." [37] In the second century, both Platonists and Pythagoreans began to incorporate into their philosophies demonology and oriental mysticism that influenced later Greek thought. [38] Jones observes that Lucian's treatment of philosophy is both a central feature of his works and one of the most paradoxical: "When he aims his satire at targets such as religious belief or magic, he often does so by making philosophy their defender or representative; when he mocks vices like hypocrisy or venality, he often incorporates them in philosophers." [39] Lucian manages to skewer most of the different schools of philosophy. He is relatively lenient with the Epicureans, whereas their traditional enemies, the Stoics, are probably his favorite target. [40] The Platonists and Pythagoreans do not fare well, particularly in the *Philopseudes*. The character Ion, a Platonist, is one of the most gullible in the dialogue, and the Pythagorean Arignotos tells the most exaggerated story of them all. Much of the *Philopseudes* may be seen as a satire on contemporary philosophers as well as on popular superstition. [41] In the egocentric character of Arignotos, Lucian has taken the opportunity to satirize not only popular superstition but philosophy as well—two objectionable items combined in one character.

Though Lucian's haunted-house story resembles Pliny's, it is far more similar in intent to the tale in Plautus's *Mostellaria*. There is a strong possibility that Lucian may have known the story of the haunted house as a theme from New Comedy, preserved in Plautus's play. [42] This comparison has been oddly neglected, considering that both Plautus and Lucian satirize *deisidaimonia*. The difficulty may lie in the fact that these authors go in opposite directions to achieve the same end. Plautus's Tranio reduces Theopropides to the typical *deisidaimon,* one who is afraid of polluting himself through contact with the dead. The philosophers in Lucian's dialogue, on the other hand, positively revel in superstitions of all kinds—they are fascinated by mysticism. Far from shunning contact with the dead, Arignotos can hardly wait to let the ghost get at him. Plautus achieves his comic effects by deviating from what seems to have been one fairly popular narrative structure for haunted-house stories, whereas Lucian achieves his satirical effects by exaggerating that same structure. In both cases, establishing a folkloric context for these ghost stories helps us to understand what the authors have done.

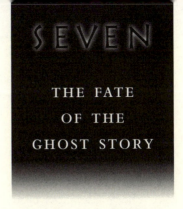

SEVEN

THE FATE OF THE GHOST STORY

LUCIAN'S *PHILOPSEUDES* MAY HAVE BEEN MODELED AFTER PLATONIC dialogues, but later gatherings where supernatural tales are told have been modeled after this dialogue of Lucian: "The idea of people gathering together to relate their supernatural experiences is now a commonplace one, but it was Lucian in his humorous dialogue *Philopseudes* who first described such a group, almost 2,000 years ago." [1] People now gather to tell ghost stories at slumber parties, or around campfires—not to mention at meetings of the many official groups formed for such purposes. These gatherings have also found a niche in supernatural literature. Mary Shelley, for example, describes the rainy-day quarantine that led to the creation of *Frankenstein:* "It proved a wet, ungenial summer, and incessant rain often confined us for days to the house. Some volumes of ghost stories translated from the German into French fell into our hands. . . . 'We will each write a ghost story,' said Lord Byron, and his proposition was acceded to." [2] Henry James introduces the supernatural narrative in *The Turn of the Screw* as one of several being told among a group gathered for just that purpose on Christmas Eve: the previous story "had held us, round the fire, sufficiently breathless." [3]

Various modern ghost stories, both humorous and serious, ultimately owe many of their elements to the ancient tales, particularly Pliny's narrative of the haunted house at Athens. This is true not only of legends collected orally, such as in the works of Solomon and Dégh, but of supernatural literature by some of the best ghost-story writers, many of whom had had classical educations and had probably read Pliny in the original Latin.

For example, in the works of modern ghost-story writers, we often find the same kind of protagonist: a thoughtful, scholarly man facing the supernatural alone. This learned protagonist is evident in Arthur Machen's "The Bowmen." The story takes place during World War I, at a battle in which the English are losing badly to the Germans. One English soldier, who "happened to know Latin and other useless things," desperately uttered the motto *Adsit Anglis Sanctus Georgius* ("May St. George help the English!") while firing at the Germans:

> As the Latin scholar uttered his invocation he felt something between a shudder and an electric shock pass through his body. . . . He heard, or seemed to hear, thousands shouting: "St. George! St. George!" . . . And as the soldier heard these voices he saw before him beyond the trench, a long line of shapes, with a shining about them. They were like men who drew the bow, and with another shout their cloud of arrows flew singing and tingling through the air towards the German hosts. . . . [He] knew that St. George had brought his Agincourt bowmen to help the English.[4]

In this case, as in Pliny and Lucian, the protagonist's learning has provided the way out of a crisis. The educated status of both the fictional character and the author himself also lends the story credibility, as we have seen with the stories from antiquity. This case provides an extreme example. Machen was indirectly describing the retreat from Mons, and his story apparently started a legend: it was believed that during the war, ghostly Agincourt bowmen really had come to the aid of the British. In an unusual reversal, a written story led to an oral tradition.[5] Machen explained, "The Bowmen of my story have become 'The Angels of Mons' . . . I credit none of the 'Angels of Mons' legends, partly because I see, or think I see, their derivation from my own idle fiction."[6] He continues, "[The story] had no foundation in fact of any kind . . . it had no foundation in rumour," but "variants of my tale began to be told as authentic histories."[7]

More evident in modern stories, however, is the tension between philosophical or scientific skepticism and popular belief, the tension between what science thinks it can explain and what remains unknown or inexplicable. The educated protagonists of modern ghost stories are more likely to meet trouble or even death because of their willingness to face the supernatural, believing it can be explained by scientific causes. This theme was particularly favored by M. R. James (1862–1936), one of the foremost ghost-story writers of the past century, whose protagonists were nearly always scholars, often even antiquaries. One of his best-known (and best-titled) stories, "Oh, Whistle, and I'll Come to You, My Lad," concerns a professor of "ontography" who finds an old whistle with the inscription QUIS EST ISTE QUI VENIT? "I ought to be able to make it out," he says to himself, "but I suppose I am a little rusty in my Latin. . . . It ought to mean, 'Who is this who is coming?' Well, the best way to find out is evidently to whistle for him."[8] The professor comes to regret his curiosity upon meeting the ghostly visitant summoned by the whistle, and probably wishes he had paid more attention to the pejorative connotations of *iste*.[9]

The chain-rattling ghost, so crucial to Pliny's story, became a favorite of British writers,[10] many of whom were aware that this "old-fashioned phenomenon of clanking chains derived from classical superstition"[11]—though it is hard to say whether or how closely the modern authors read Pliny. Note, for example, how Dickens describes the entrance of Marley's ghost in *A Christmas Carol:*

> The bells ceased as they had begun, together. They were succeeded by a clanking noise, deep down below; as if some person were dragging a heavy chain over the casks in the wine-merchant's cellar. Scrooge then remembered to have heard that ghosts in haunted houses were described as dragging chains.
>   The cellar-door flew open with a booming sound, and then he heard the noise much louder, on the floors below; then coming up the stairs; then coming straight toward his door. . . . Without a pause, it came on through the heavy door, and passed into the room before his eyes. Upon its coming in, the dying flame leaped up, as though it cried "I know him! Marley's Ghost!" and fell again.[12]

Dickens draws out the suspense by having the noise move closer and closer to Scrooge's room, up to the door, and then through it, an effect used by Pliny two thousand years earlier. Like Pliny, Dickens places great emphasis on the chain this ghost drags: "The chain he drew was clasped about his middle. It was long, and wound about him like a tail; and it was made (for Scrooge observed it closely) of cashboxes, keys, padlocks, ledgers, deeds, and heavy purses wrought in steel."[13] Unlike Pliny, Dickens offers an explanation for the chains—a metaphorical explanation—as Scrooge inquires of Marley, "You are fettered. . . . Tell me why?" The ghost replies, "I wear the chain I forged in life. . . . I made it link by link, and yard by yard; I girded it on of my own free will, and of my own free will I wore it."[14] Marley refers to his own miserliness and lack of charity. Scrooge, meanwhile, tries to be calm and rational; compare Athenodorus two thousand years earlier. Scrooge doubts his senses, because "a little thing affects them. A slight disorder of the stomach makes them cheats." Scrooge pleads the popular theory of hallucinations, that ghosts and other specters are caused by indigestion.[15] Such an explanation echoes interpretations of dreams going back as far as Aristotle, who argued that dreams are the result of natural disorders or other stimuli on the mind. Like Athenodorus, who followed the old man's ghost, Scrooge eventually allows himself to be led by the ghosts of Christmas Past, Present, and Future.

In his description of Marley's ghost, Dickens was not the only British writer of ghost stories who owed a debt to the classical writers. Here, for example, is a scene from Oscar Wilde's "The Canterville Ghost":

> At eleven o'clock the family retired, and by half-past all the lights were out. Some time after, Mr. Otis was awakened by a curious noise in the corridor, outside his room. It sounded like the clank of metal, and seemed to be coming nearer every moment. He got up at once, struck a match, and looked at the time. It was exactly one o'clock. He was quite calm, and felt his pulse, which was not at all feverish. The strange noise still continued, and with it he heard distinctly the sound of footsteps. He put on his slippers, took a small oblong phial out of his dressing-case, and opened the door. Right in front of him he saw, in the wan moonlight, an old man of terrible aspect. His eyes were as red burning coals; long grey hair fell over his shoulders in matted coils; his garments, which were of antique cut, were soiled and ragged, and from his wrists and ankles hung heavy manacles and rusty gyves.[16]

Whether Wilde was intentionally following Pliny or not, several close parallels with Pliny's story are immediately obvious. The ghost here appears late at night. The initial disturbance is a noise that sounds like clanking metal and comes closer and closer, which parallels Pliny's description, "you could hear . . . the clanking of chains, first from far off, then from close by" (*strepitus vinculorum longius primo deinde e proximo reddebatur,* 7.27.5). The person to whom the ghost appears is calm and rational, as was Athenodorus. The noise continues; although it is not described as increasing in volume, the placement of this phrase parallels Pliny's, "Then the din grew even louder" (*tum crebescere fragor,* 7.27.8). Light, in this case moonlight, is needed in this story so that the ghost can be seen, as in Pliny (and Lucian). The physical appearance of the ghost might have been drawn straight from Pliny: an old man with long, matted hair (*promissa barba, horrenti capillo*) and dirty clothes (*squalore confectus*), with chains—described separately—on his arms and legs (*cruribus compedes, manibus catenas,* 7.27.5). Wilde's passage continues, however, in an entirely different tone:

> "My dear sir," said Mr. Otis, "I really must insist on your oiling those chains, and have brought you for that purpose a small bottle of the Tammany Rising Sun Lubricator. It is said to be completely efficacious upon one application, and there are several testimonials to that effect on the wrapper from some of our most eminent native divines. I shall leave it here

for you by the bedroom candles, and will be happy to supply you with
more should you require it." With these words the United States Minis-
ter laid the bottle down on a marble table, and, closing his door, retired
to rest.

As a satire of ghost stories, this differs from Lucian's. Here, the unexpected
shift in tone as Mr. Otis turns the tables on the ghost has a much greater
effect, at least on the modern reader, than the constant exaggeration employed by Lucian. Even so, Wilde's satire works along similar lines to
Lucian's: both make fun of the type of person involved, with the audacious
American and his cures replacing the Pythagorean philosopher and his
spells. Where Lucian relies on exaggeration of the ghost's powers and appearance for satiric effect, Wilde in these particular passages does not,
though he does so elsewhere in the story, with the ghost appearing variously as "Martin the Maniac, or The Masked Mystery," "The Vampire
Monk, or, The Bloodless Benedictine," and in other such roles.[17] In a shift
of tone from the satirical to the sentimental, Wilde's ending, too, reflects
similar endings found in classical authors. The ghost, who has admitted to
killing his wife and paying dearly for it, haunts the house because he has
not received proper burial and his spirit cannot rest. It falls to the young
daughter of the American family, a more serious character than her father,
to discover the ghost's resting place and to lead the family to a secret chamber shown to her by the ghost:

They found themselves in a little low room, with a vaulted ceiling, and
one tiny grated window. Imbedded in the wall was a huge iron ring, and
chained to it was a gaunt skeleton, that was stretched out at full length on
the stone floor, and seemed to be trying to grasp with its long fleshless fingers an old-fashioned trencher and ewer, that were placed just out of its
reach.

As in Pliny's story from nearly two thousand years earlier, the bones are
discovered in chains. In this case, Wilde has explained the reason for the
chains. The punishment inflicted on the prisoner has classical overtones,
ultimately deriving from the myth of Tantalus. The ghost has more than
atoned for the rash act of killing his wife in a fit of anger. The family gives
the remains a proper and very elaborate burial ceremony, and Canterville
Chase is haunted no more.

There are many similarities not only in the narrative structures of ancient
and modern ghost stories, but also in the underlying themes and imagery,

particularly liminal imagery. In his study of American ghost legends, Jones observes, "For some reason, the dead seem to be especially interested in doors and windows. Doors in their houses are opened by no earthly hands; they slam shut when there is not wind blowing; they resist all mortal efforts to keep them locked." [18] Ghosts are unusually fond of stairways as well. [19] That ghosts should appear most often in connection with doors, windows, and stairways is not so surprising when we consider that all three locations represent the marginal or "liminal" status in which ghosts exist. Ghosts are "betwixt and between" this world and the next: they are no longer living beings, but have not yet fully crossed over into the land of the dead, because they have suffered violent deaths or have not been buried properly. They have not, in other words, had their rite of passage. [20] Doors and windows are both thresholds, passageways into or out of the house, while stairways are neither one floor of a house nor another, but rather are passageways between them.

Such imagery is common in antiquity as well. Several portents recorded by Suetonius, for example, reflect the symbolism of doorways as passages to the next world. He reports that on the night before Caesar's murder, the doors of the room in which Caesar and his wife Calpurnia were sleeping "suddenly opened by themselves" (*subito cubiculi fores sponte patuerunt, Iul.* 81.3). Krauss explains, "Some unseen spirit, operating by the wish of heaven, had opened it and had thereby signified that Caesar would soon be carried forth in his final sleep." [21] A similar portent occurred to Nero in his last days: "From the Mausoleum, whose doors had opened by themselves, a voice was heard calling him by name" (*de Mausoleo, sponte foribus patefactis, exaudita vox est nomine eum cientis*). [22]

The time of day when ghosts appear also reflects their liminal status. Some types of apparition, such as warning apparitions, appear at midday, while others appear at midnight: the former is a boundary between morning and evening, the latter between one day and the next. And many people report seeing ghosts during liminal states of consciousness, at the edge of sleeping and waking, if not actually in dreams. The monosandalism satirized in Lucian's story of Eucrates' dead wife represents the threshold between the material and spirit worlds, while the shape-shifting of the black daimon in the haunted house at Corinth is liminal "insofar as it is hybrid." [23] Johnston points out,

> The Greeks, Romans, and many other ancient civilizations regarded both natural and man-made liminal points of all kinds—doors, gates, rivers and frontiers, as well as crossroads—as uncertain places, requiring special

rituals . . . because of their lack of association with either of two extremes, liminal points eluded categorization—a threshold was neither in nor out of the house, a crossroad was part of neither road A nor road B.[24]

Even the haunted house itself embodies a liminal quality, as it reflects the ambiguous area between nature and culture.[25] Life and death themselves are both acceptable states for the soul; it is the margin between them, the state of limbo in which restless souls find themselves, that causes problems.[26]

Liminal imagery of all kinds is particularly clear in Pliny's ghost stories. The apparition of the old man, which appears in the middle of the night, moves up to the threshold of the room in which Athenodorus is studying: "Now it was at the threshold—now it was inside the room" (*iam ut in limine, iam ut intra limine*). While this reflects the marginal status of the ghost, for Athenodorus it also signals the ghost's movement from the realm of the imagination into the realm of reality. Athenodorus follows the ghost into the courtyard (*aream,* 7.27.10), a place neither outside nor inside but partaking of both. Here the bones are found, reinforcing the idea that the restless spirit was neither part of this world nor yet part of the next. Similarly, Pliny's slave-boy reports that two ghostly figures "came in through the window and left by the same way they had come" (*venerunt per fenestras . . . et qua venerant recesserunt,* 7.27.13). On the one hand, this naturally suggests that the figures were not ghosts at all, since ghosts should not need to climb in and out of windows. On the other hand, this detail in the story is consistent with the liminal imagery associated with ghost stories. Ghosts have an affinity for such entryways, as part of their attempts to cross the threshold between worlds.

The short tale of the supernatural first found its place in fiction in the time of the Greeks and Romans, but despite the lasting influence of authors such as Plautus, Pliny, and Lucian, it would be centuries before the ghost story became popular enough to be identified as a distinct genre of literature. Although weird tales appeared in medieval ballads and Arthurian legends, and ghosts were frequently characters in Elizabethan drama,[27] the modern ghost story is generally agreed to have grown more directly out of Gothic novels such as Horace Walpole's *The Castle of Otranto* (1764) and Matthew Lewis's *The Monk* (1796), both of which relied heavily on supernatural details. Ominous ghosts walked the halls of cavernous mansions, though the ghosts in such novels generally played a secondary role.[28] This seemingly sudden flourishing of supernatural fiction in the eighteenth century was partially a reaction to the Age of Reason, a backlash resulting in a revival of interest in the irrational.[29]

The popularity of the Gothic novel gave the supernatural a home in modern literature. But in the nineteenth century the short story, rather than the novel, became the medium for supernatural tales,[30] and the Victorian ghost story even had a distinct "anti-Gothic" character.[31] Whereas the Gothic ghost story typically emphasized epic settings and lurid action, the Victorian often had a quiet domestic setting and more realistic protagonists, and aimed not so much to shock as to unsettle its readers. Where the Gothic in literature arose as a reaction to the rationalism and skepticism of the Enlightenment, the Victorian interest in the supernatural seemed to be a reaction to the Industrial Revolution and the unexpectedly rapid social and cultural changes that accompanied it, a reaction evident not only in nineteenth-century literature but also in the concurrent popularity of spiritualism and parapsychology in general. The ghost story as a genre reached its height in England and America in the late nineteenth and early twentieth century with the works of writers such as Joseph Sheridan Le Fanu, Arthur Machen, Henry James, M. R. James, Algernon Blackwood, E. Nesbit, and Edith Wharton, to name only a few.[32]

The shock, cynicism, and suffering generated by World War I alienated readers of the genre, and although many writers, such as Blackwood, M. R. James, Wharton, H. Russell Wakefield, A. M. Burrage, and E. F. Benson, were still producing good ghost stories, the genre seemed to have passed its prime. The horrors of World War II and the atomic bomb by far overshadowed anything still appearing in ghost stories.[33] The years after World War II saw the rise of a new genre, science fiction, as various developments in science continued to affect adversely the popularity of supernatural stories. Candles and their eerie shadows flickered out as electricity flooded rooms with light.[34] Scientific advances have led us to believe that nearly everything can be explained in scientific terms, and unlike the ancient Greeks and Romans, we no longer think of the "supernatural as part of nature."

Still, the ghost story is not likely to disappear any time soon. Ghost stories "have always maintained an adaptable relationship with the contemporary world. And, of course, a belief in ghosts—even the literary pretence of a belief—is a peculiarly resilient one, culturally speaking, and provides a potent fictional dynamic that seems continually attractive to both writers and readers."[35] And there is always an audience for a good story. So we find, in the late twentieth century, that supernatural fiction is still alive and well. The haunted house remains popular in literature, particularly in novels such as Shirley Jackson's *The Haunting of Hill House* (1959), Richard Matheson's *Hell House* (1971), and Stephen King's *The Shining* (1978), all descendants of the eighteenth-century Gothic novel. The opening of Jackson's novel immediately sets forth the tension between light and dark, waking and dreaming, rational and irrational:

> No live organism can continue for long to exist sanely under conditions of absolute reality; even larks and katydids are supposed, by some, to dream. Hill House, not sane, stood by itself against its hills, holding darkness within; it had stood so for eighty years and might stand for eighty more. Within, walls continued upright, bricks met neatly, floors were firm, and doors were sensibly shut; silence lay steadily against the wood and stone of Hill House, and whatever walked there, walked alone.[36]

In Jackson's novel, as well as those of Matheson and King, the house itself becomes a major character in the story, even as the haunting is used as a background to explore family relationships and the human psyche.[37]

At its core, the ghost story, based on folk legends and arising from oral traditions, reflects religious beliefs concerning the importance of a proper burial and the survival of the spirit after death. The dead have a need to rest in peace, while the living have a need to believe in an afterlife. Even humorous ghost stories, from Plautus to Oscar Wilde, can represent a way to deal with the disturbing reality of death. Meanwhile, much more could be said about the folklore elements in ghost stories, as well as about their literary qualities. As Sullivan observes, "What unifies all of the better stories . . . is an unbroken sense of mystery and enigma."[38] Ghost legends and literature depend on suggestion and connotation, which is what makes even Pliny's very short story so effective. "Supernatural horror is usually more convincing when suggested or evoked than when explicitly documented,"[39] and such "explicit documentation" as that found in Lucian's story lends itself better to humor than to horror. In tales of the supernatural we find a fascination with darkness and irrationality and a focus on liminal states of consciousness and perception, all of which might be illuminated through a continued study of ghost stories both ancient and modern.

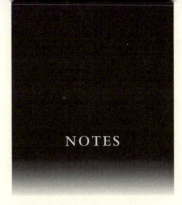

Introduction

1. Luck [1985] 1992:169.
2. Guiley 1992:160.
3. Ibid.: 161.
4. Tyrrell [1953] 1970:44.
5. Sullivan 1986:168. See also discussion in Myers 1961:207ff.
6. See Krauss 1930. Also, both then and now, there are physical explanations for such phenomena, having to do with the weather, volcanic activity, and other occurrences in nature.
7. Particularly Cumont [1922] 1923 and 1949; Rohde 1925; Lattimore [1942] 1962; Toynbee 1971; Vermeule 1979; Hopkins 1983; Garland 1985.
8. Technically, the term "underworld" is inaccurate for Homer's Land of the Dead, which is at the end of the known world but not literally under the ground. But it is still the most popular term for describing various afterlife abodes, and so I use it in that very generalized sense throughout this book.
9. Browne [1658] 1977:62. In quoting from Browne, I have retained the original spellings.
10. Hopkins 1983:227.
11. Ibid.: 226.
12. Nardi 1960 and 1975–1976a and b; Radermacher 1979. Though Nardi, in all these works, does not focus on ghosts in drama, he considers Plautus's *Mostellaria* in his discussion because it contains a haunted-house story.
13. Hickman 1938:13.
14. Collison-Morley [1912] 1968:64.
15. Sherwin-White [1966] 1985:436.
16. Penzoldt 1952; Briggs 1977; Lovecraft [1945] 1973.
17. Lloyd-Jones 1982:293.
18. Collison-Morley [1912] 1968:17.
19. Dundes 1965.
20. Johnston 1994:100.
21. Scarborough [1917] 1967:87.

Chapter One

1. Hansen 1988:1121. He goes on to explain that the term "folklore" came into being only in the mid-nineteenth century.

2. Brunvand 1981:3; also Bascom 1965:3.

3. Brunvand 1981:3.

4. Bascom (1965:3) specifically calls them *prose* narratives. Myth can also be presented in verse form.

5. Ibid.: 4–5. Bascom notes that in some cultures, only two kinds of prose narrative are distinguished: true and fictional, with folktales recognized as fiction, and "myth-legend" blended into one category of nonfiction. But he observes that in Euro-American folklore, all three categories are distinct.

6. Grider 1997:2. See also discussions in Utley (1976) and Lüthi (1976).

7. Lovecraft ([1945] 1973:20) observes that it is in poetry that we first encounter the permanent entry of the weird into standard literature, citing the Scandinavian Eddas, *Beowulf,* and the Nibelung tales. But he adds, "Most of the ancient instances, curiously enough, are in prose; as the werewolf incident in Petronius, the gruesome passages in Apuleius, the brief but celebrated letter of Pliny the Younger to Sura, and the odd compilation *On Wonderful Events* by the Emperor Hadrian's Greek freedman, Phlegon."

8. Brunvand 1981:3.

9. Ibid.: 12.

10. Dundes 1993:xi.

11. Brunvand 1981:xi.

12. Ibid.: xii.

13. Ibid.: 4.

14. L. C. Jones 1959:162.

15. Brunvand 1981:4.

16. Solomon and Solomon 1981:2.

17. Ibid.: 3–4.

18. Ibid.: 4.

19. Halpert 1971:54. On humor in ghost stories, see also Sarkissian 1985. Sarkissian looks specifically at humor in Oscar Wilde's "The Canterville Ghost" and H. G. Wells's "The Inexperienced Ghost."

20. Ibid.

21. See Dégh and Vázsonyi 1976.

22. *HN* 28.188: *invenio aput auctores his qui lentigines habeant negari magice sacrificiorum usum,* "I find in my sources that participation in magic rituals is forbidden to those who have freckles."

23. *HN* 30.16: *lentiginem habentibus non obsequi numina aut cerni,* "Divine beings do not obey those who have freckles, and are not seen by them."

24. Halliday 1930:122.

25. Johnston 1991:223. See also Johnston 1990.

26. See Rohde 1925:52 n. 72.

27. Sussman 1987:129.

28. See Fontenrose [1978] 1981:130; Faraone 1991b, esp. 180–89; and Larson 1995:134.

29. Many of the beliefs under discussion here still exist in modern Greece, such as the beliefs that ghosts haunt crossroads, that iron can protect against spirits, that dogs can sense spirits, and that ghosts disappear at cockcrow, "for the rooster separates the day which 'God made for man' from the night, which belongs to the spirits and which is for some the Bad Hour itself" (Blum and Blum 1970:123; see also pp. 124, 138, and 341 there).

30. Solomon and Solomon 1981:26.

31. Gaster [1969] 1981, 1:309. See Krappe 1943:391–401 for examples from many cultures, including those cited here from ancient Greece.

32. Krappe 1943:401.

33. μῆνιν ἄειδε, θεά, Πηληιάδεω Ἀχιλῆος . . . / πολλὰς δ' ἰφθίμους ψυχὰς Ἄιδι προίαψεν / ἡρώων, αὐτοὺς δὲ ἑλώρια τεῦχε κύνεσσιν / οἰωνοῖσι. It may be for this reason, too, that a monstrous dog (Cerberus) was said to guard the entrance to Hades.

34. Solomon and Solomon 1981:26. See also MacKenzie 1971:48–58; and Drexler 1894–97.

35. As Sherwin-White ([1966] 1985:436) notes: "The time is just after midday, as Tacitus confirms." Winkler (1980:159 n. 11) argues that some ancient authors mention ghosts that appear at midday, but these ghosts usually appear in a sacred grove so thick and shady that no daylight enters, and the point is not that noon is dangerous but that in such places it is always virtually night (Luc. 3.423–25; Stat. *Theb.* 4.438–41; and the example from Lucian *Philops.* 22–24 given below). Most of the other references to such a belief are based on the principle that rural deities rest and take their swimming break or siesta at midday, just as the shepherds do, and that they do not like to be disturbed.

36. But it is not true for all cases of warning apparitions. The phantom that appears to Brutus comes in the middle of the night, while his tent is dimly lit, and the camp is silent (Plut. *Brut.* 36.3).

37. Edith Wharton sustains an entire ghost story with a similar narrative effect. In her "Afterward," an American couple buys a house in England that is supposed to be haunted, but by a ghost that no one ever recognizes as such, prompting the following exchange (1937:71):

> "But what in the world constitutes a ghost except the fact of its being known for one?"
> "I can't say. But that's the story."
> "That there's a ghost, but that nobody knows it's a ghost?"
> "Well—not till afterward, at any rate."
> "Till afterward?"
> "Not till long long afterward."

38. Winkler 1980:158–59.

39. The relationship between ghosts and dreams will be discussed in more detail below.

40. Solomon and Solomon 1981:26.

41. Brown 1979:55.

42. Jenkins [1982] 1984:424, with further references.

43. Hill 1891, 3:349. This brings to mind Boswell's description of his first meeting with Johnson: "At last, on Monday the 16th of May, when I was sitting in Mr. Davies's back-parlour . . . Johnson unexpectedly came into the shop; and Mr. Davies having perceived him through the glass-door in the room in which we were sitting, advancing towards us,—he announced his aweful approach to me, somewhat in the manner of an actor in the part of Horatio, when he addresses Hamlet on the appearance of his father's ghost, 'Look, my Lord, it comes'" (ibid., 1:453).

44. *Brut.* 36.3–4: ὁ δὲ συλλογιζόμενός τι καὶ σκοπῶν πρὸς ἑαυτὸν ἔδοξεν αἰσθέσθαι τινὸς εἰσιόντος. ἀποβλέψας δὲ πρὸς τὴν εἴσοδον ὁρᾷ δεινὴν καὶ ἀλλόκοτον ὄψιν ἐκφύλου σώματος καὶ φοβεροῦ, σιωπῇ παρεστῶτος αὐτῷ. τολμήσας δὲ ἐρέσθαι, Τίς ποτ' ὤν, εἶπεν, ἀνθρώπων ἢ θεῶν, ἢ τί βουλόμενος ἥκεις ὡς ἡμᾶς; Ὑποφθέγγεται δ' αὐτῷ τὸ φάσμα· Ὁ σός, ὦ Βροῦτε, δαίμων κακός· ὄψει δέ με περὶ Φιλίππους.

45. Elpenor can speak without drinking the blood because he is not yet a true inhabitant of Hades; Teiresias, by virtue of his powers, also does not need to drink before speaking.

46. L. C. Jones 1959:19; Sullivan 1986:170. We also have examples of doomed characters threatening that they will haunt their persecutors: at Horace *Epode* 5.91–93, a young boy being tortured to death by the witch Canidia threatens that his ghost will haunt her, and Dido, about to be abandoned by Aeneas, makes a similar threat (Verg. *Aen.* 4.385–86).

47. *Aen.* 1.353–57: *ipsa sed in somnis inhumati venit imago / coniugis ora modis attolens pallida miris; . . . / caecumque domus scelus omne retexit.*

48. Apul. *Met.* 8.8: *ne in Thrasylli manum sacrilegam convenias neve sermonem conferas nec mensam accumbas nec toro adquiescas. fuge mei percussoris cruentam dexteram.* In the necromancy scene at Apuleius *Met.* 2.28–30, the spirit of a dead man is summoned back to his body specifically so that the corpse may reveal the name of his murderer.

49. Cic. *Div.* 1.27: *de Semonide, qui cum ignotum quendam proiectum mortuum vidisset eumque humavisset haberetque in animo navem conscendere, moneri visus est, ne id faceret, ab eo quem sepultura adfecerat; si navigavisset, eum naufragio esse periturum; itaque Simonidem redisse, perisse ceteros qui tum navigassent.* The story is referred to again in *Div.* 2.65–66. Pease (1920:194 n. 5) gives a parallel story from Valerius Maximus 1.7. This story is one of the earliest written examples of the "Grateful Dead" tale type. See Aarne and Thompson, tale types 505–8 (1961:171–75). Henceforth all references to Aarne and Thompson will be by "AT" tale type number and title, e.g., AT 505–8, "The Grateful Dead." See

also Gerould 1908; Liljeblad 1927; Röhrich 1981. A well-known example of this tale type is Hans Christian Andersen's story, "The Travelling Companion."

50. Luck [1985] 1992:166.

51. Cumont [1922] 1923:64.

52. Rohde 1925:162–63.

53. Ibid.: 163.

54. Collison-Morley [1912] 1968:6.

55. Versions of this story are found in Euripides' *Hecuba*, Ovid's *Metamorphoses* 13.441 ff., and Seneca's *Troades*, among others.

56. Suet. *Calig.* 59: *cadaver eius clam in hortos Lamianos asportatum et tumultuario rogo semiambustum levi caespite obrutum est, postea per sorores ab exsilio reversas erutum et crematum sepultumque. satis constat, prius quam id fieret, hortorum custodes umbris inquietatos; in ea quoque domo, in qua occubuerit, nullam noctem sine aliquo terrore transactam, donec ipsa domus incendio consumpta sit.* L. C. Jones (1959:70), having analyzed many legends of hauntings, concludes, "The one sure method [for eliminating ghosts from a house] is to burn the house down."

57. C. Russell [1980] 1981:132.

58. Ibid.

59. Strubbe 1991:33.

60. Gager 1992:177; Gager considers the imprecations a subcategory of *defixiones*, lead tablets inscribed with a curse and then placed in a grave or nailed to the wall of a tomb. For further discussions of the distinctions among funerary imprecations, epitaphs, and *defixiones*, see Strubbe 1991:33; Faraone 1991a.

61. Lattimore [1942] 1962:109.

62. C. Russell [1980] 1981:132–33.

63. Van Gennep 1960:146 ff. See also Pentikäinen 1968:50–51.

64. Suet. *Ner.* 34: *saepe confessus exagitari se materna specie verberibusque Furiarum ac taedis ardentibus. quin et facto per Magos sacro evocare Manes et exorare temptavit.*

65. Nero's generally unbalanced mind seemed to be plagued by ghosts at every turn. Tacitus describes how, after Agrippina's murder, "There were those who believed that Nero heard the sound of a trumpet and of lamentations echoing in the high hills at his mother's grave" (*Ann.* 14.10). Apart from his mother's restless spirit, Nero had also encountered ghosts when he tried to dig a canal across the Isthmus of Corinth. When the first workers broke the earth, blood spurted out, groans and bellowing were heard, and many phantoms appeared (Dio Cass. 62.16). Nero abandoned the project.

66. Suet. *Otho* 7: *dicitur ea nocte per quietem pavefactus gemitus maximos edidisse repertusque a concursantibus humi ante lectum iacens per omnia piaculorum genera Manes Galbae . . . propitiare temptasse.*

67. A similar story is told of the emperor Constantius II (A.D. 337–361): he had terrible nightmares, in which he dreamed he was being attacked by the shrieking ghosts of the multitudes he had killed. It seemed to him that the

ghosts seized him and threw him into the claws of the Furies (Amm. Marc. 14.11.17).

68. After his death, Pausanias himself did not rest easy. His ghost seems to have haunted the Spartans until his spirit was appeased with the offering of two bronze statues. See discussions in Fontenrose [1978] 1981: 129–30 and Faraone 1991b: 184–87.

69. Rohde 1925: 168.

70. Burkert 1983: 216.

71. Rohde 1925: 168. He offers several different explanations for why pitch and hawthorn were thought to have this apotropaic effect.

72. On this formula and the *Kēres* (Κῆρες), see Rohde 1925: 44 n. 10, 168, and 199 n. 100. Burkert 1985: 240.

73. Frazer 1929, 2: 431ff.

74. Beans have many associations with ghosts. The Greeks associated beans with the souls of the dead and the transmigration of the soul (metempsychosis). The Pythagoreans refused to eat beans on this account. The Romans, too, considered beans sacred and used them in various festivals for the dead such as this one. Pliny the Elder tells us that the souls of the dead were believed to be contained in beans, and for this reason beans are used in memorial sacrifices to dead relatives (*HN* 18.118). Frazer (1929, 4: 38) suggests that the ghosts were supposed to accept the beans as substitutes for the living members of the family, whom they might otherwise have harmed, and that for this same reason the Romans threw beans into graves "for the safety of men," in the hope that the dead would accept the offering and leave the living alone. See also Burkert 1972: 183–84. On Ovid's presentation of the Parentalia and Lemuria, see Phillips 1992.

75. Scullard 1981: 180–81.

76. Lawson 1964: 505. By Shakespeare's time, it was a common superstition that lights burned dim, or blue, in the presence of a ghost or evil spirit; thus, just prior to the entrance of Caesar's ghost, Brutus can remark, "How ill this taper burns!" (*Julius Caesar,* 4.3.274). See Dorsch [1955] 1983: 111. The scene may also have been influenced by Plutarch's description of Brutus's tent as dimly lit (*Brut.* 36.3). See also the examples in Opie and Tatem 1989: 53.

77. Frazer 1929, 2: 434.

78. Winkler 1980: 160–61.

79. W. M. S. Russell [1980] 1981: 196.

80. Winkler does note one specific exception, from Heliodoros's *Aithiopika,* which he suggests exemplifies the Greco-Roman attitudes toward actual black persons (1980: 162 and 162 n. 28).

81. W. M. S. Russell [1980] 1981: 196.

82. Winkler 1980: 161 n. 26, citing Silius Italicus 13.447; Stat. *Theb.* 8.5 ff. But cf. Prop. 4.7.2: "And the pale ghost escapes the dying embers" (*luridaque evictos effugit umbra rogos*).

83. Winkler 1980:162.

84. Cf. also *larvalis* applied to skeletons: Sen. *Ep.* 24.8; Apul. *Apol.* 63 (Winkler 1980:163).

85. Winkler 1980:162, noting that the Greek examples of white ghosts are far fewer than Latin examples.

86. Ibid.: 163 and 163 n. 42. The white sheets so popular in American folklore may represent the burial shroud.

87. Krauss 1930:155.

88. *Philops.* 25: ἐφίσταταί μοι νεανίας ἐγρηγορότι πάγκαλος λευκὸν ἱμάτιον περιβεβλημένος, εἶτα ἀναστήσας ἄγει διά τινος χάσματος εἰς τὸν Ἅιδην.

89. The importance of ghosts' descriptions is not necessarily so much whether they are black or white as that they are not any *color.* That is, the essence of death is the absence of what characterizes life. For spiritlike figures in white, cf. Plato *Crito* 44b, the woman in white who appears to Socrates in a dream to reveal the day of his death. On this and similar episodes, see Dodds 1951:107.

90. Winkler 1980:163.

91. W. M. S. Russell [1980] 1981:196.

92. Winkler 1980:164 n. 45.

93. This instance is discussed in detail by Stanford (1940).

94. One type of ghost we do not find in the remaining literature from antiquity is the acephalic ghost. This may be because decapitation was not usually instituted as a punishment for crimes, though it was known and practiced at some times, particularly in Rome. It was evidently not a common form of murder. See Voisin 1984; also Lucian *Philops.* 29. In any case, we have no ancient equivalent for the headless ghost of Anne Boleyn roaming the Tower of London, or for Washington Irving's Headless Horseman. For an interesting Jungian approach to the symbolic meaning of faceless and headless apparitions, see Jaffé 1979:133–37. The lack of headless ghosts is particularly interesting given the number of severed heads that speak, such as the head of Orpheus, which continues to sing after his body has been torn limb from limb (Ovid *Met.* 11.51–53); the severed head of a child, which utters prophecies (Phlegon *Mir.* 2.11); and the severed head of the general Publius, which also utters prophecies (Phlegon *Mir.* 3.14).

95. Attic red-figure *pelike,* c. 440 B.C. Boston Museum of Fine Arts, no. 34.79, by the Lykaon Painter. Often on Greek vases we find depictions of winged souls or soul-birds, but these are not the ghosts of specific individuals. See Vermeule 1979, passim.

96. *Aen.* 2.270 ff.:

> in somnis, ecce, ante oculos maestissimus Hector
> visus adesse mihi largosque effundere fletus
> raptatus bigis ut quondam, aterque cruento

> pulvere perque pedes traiectus lora tumentis. . . .
> squalentem barbam et concretos sanguine crinis
> vulneraque illa gerens.

97. *nox erat: ante torum visa est adstare sororis / squalenti Dido sanguinulenta coma / et "fuge, ne dubita, maestum fuge" dicere "tectum!"* (*Fasti* 3.639–41). Silius Italicus (8.166–83) gives Dido's ghost a longer speech but a less gory description ("Dido, extremely troubled, with a sad face," *tristi cum Dido aegerrima vultu*, 166.) I thank Mary Davisson for bringing the Ovid passage to my attention.

98. Apul. *Met.* 8.8: *umbra illa misere trucidati Tlepolemi, sanie cruentam et pallore deformem attollens faciem, quietem pudicam interpellat uxoris.* Seneca was particularly fond of gore, and described even ghosts who appeared offstage in gruesome detail, as the ghost of Laius from the *Oedipus.* See Hickman 1938: 87–113.

99. Winkler 1980: 163.

100. Luck [1985] 1992: 170; Dodds 1973: 205.

101. Bierce 1941: 116.

102. Tyrrell [1953] 1970: 72–73.

103. Ibid.: 8–9.

104. Ibid.: passim.

105. C. Russell [1980] 1981: 118.

106. Lattimore [1942] 1962: 46 n. 185. See also Lang [1897] 1970.

107. On incubation, see Rohde 1925: 92–93, 133; and Dodds 1951: 110ff.

108. Dodds 1951: 105, noting that this usage is particularly common in Herodotus.

109. W. M. S. Russell [1980] 1981: 203–5.

110. For a detailed discussion of Lucretius' attitude toward death, see Segal 1990.

111. Cic. *Div.* 1.27: *cum duo quidam Arcades familiares iter una facerent et Megaram venissent, alterum ad coponem devertisse, ad hospitem alterum. qui ut cenati quiescerent, concubia nocte visum esse in somnis ei, qui erat in hospitio, illum alterum orare ut subveniret, quod sibi a copone interitus pararetur; eum primo perterritum somnio surrexisse, dein cum se conlegisset idque visum pro nihilo habendum esse duxisset recubuisse; tum ei dormienti eundem illum visum esse rogare ut, quoniam sibi vivo non subvenisset, mortem suam ne inultam esse pateretur; se interfectum in plaustrum a copone esse coniectum et supra stercus iniectum; petere ut mane ad portam adesset prius quam plaustrum ex oppido exiret. hoc vero eum somnio commotum mane bubulco praesto ad portam fuisse, quaesisse ex eo quid esset in plaustro; illum perterritum fugisse, mortuum erutum esse, cauponem re patefacta poenas dedisse.*

112. Plut. *Brut.* 37.1–3: οὐ πάντα πάσχομεν ἀληθῶς οὐδ' ὁρῶμεν, ἀλλ' ὑγρὸν μέν τι χρῆμα καὶ ἀπατηλὸν ἡ αἴσθησις, ἔτι δ' ὀξυτέρα ἡ διάνοια κινεῖν αὐτὸ καὶ μεταβάλλειν ἀπ' οὐδενὸς ὑπάρχοντος ἐπὶ πᾶσαν ἰδέαν. . . . δαίμονας δ' οὔτ' εἶναι πιθανὸν οὔτ' ὄντας ἀνθρώπων ἔχειν εἶδος ἢ φωνήν.

113. Kemper 1993: 18.

Chapter Two

1. Wendland 1911:50–51.

2. Knight 1970:117. For a good survey of werewolf stories, see Smith 1894, which includes not only Petronius but other examples of werewolf stories and beliefs in antiquity.

3. Messent 1981:16.

4. Johnston 1994:100.

5. Ibid.: 100–101.

6. Klotsche 1918:89.

7. See Luck [1985] 1992:163ff. for an extended discussion of daimonology in antiquity.

8. Less frequently used Greek words for "ghost" include εἰκών, ὄψις, and δόκησις.

9. Collison-Morley [1912] 1968:7; Winkler 1980:159 n. 15. *Lemures* and *manes* are used only in the plural. Cumont ([1922] 1923:72) observes, "These words stand for the vague conceptions formed of the shades of the dead. . . . [They] were a nameless crowd, hardly individualized." See also Jobbé-Duval 1924.

10. Frazer 1929, 1:37, with other examples, and noting that Ovid seems to regard *lemures* and *manes* as synonyms.

11. Latin terms less frequently used to describe ghosts were *facies,* which tended to refer to images seen in dreams, and *figura,* which, as we will see, was applied to the semi-divine apparitions of women.

12. Luck [1985] 1992:187. He continues: "Similarly, the German word 'Geist' has a wide range of meaning, with 'spirit' in one sense or another fitting most of them."

13. Spencer and Spencer 1992:2.

14. Tert. *De an.* 56. See discussion in Waszink 1947:565–66, with references to earlier Greek and Roman literature. The confusion is also evident, for example, in Vergil (*Aen.* 6). The crowd of *inhumata* ("unburied") have to wait a hundred years, but after that Charon will ferry them across the Styx; the infants, those who died before their time, may be unhappy but have at least been received into Hades (6.325–30, 426–30). Those who had died violently and those who were left unburied were considered especially dangerous and malevolent (Rohde 1925:210 n. 148 and 594–95). See also Pentikäinen 1968: 49, 51–55; Johnston 1995: passim.

15. Hansen 1996:65. One of the most famous modern ghost stories to employ a revenant is W. W. Jacobs's "The Monkey's Paw."

16. Hansen 1980:73; 1989; 1996:25ff. The most recent text of Phlegon is that of Giannini (1965:170–78). The story of Philinnion influenced Goethe's "Bride of Corinth" and Washington Irving's "The Tale of the German Student." See Lovecraft [1945] 1973:20 and Hansen 1996:70ff.

17. Burkert (1983:244) notes a possible earlier version of this tale type, with

the gender roles reversed, in Euripides' tragedy *Protesilaos*. The widow is unable to reconcile herself to her husband's death: she sets up an image of the dead man, and talks and cries to it. Her agony is enough to compel the dead man up out of Hades. Protesilaos appears to her and shares her bed for one night; after that, she kills herself.

18. Luck [1985] 1992:170.

19. Haining (1982:207) notes, "Revenant is often thought to be just another word for a ghost, but actually its original meaning was to describe any being that returned from the dead." Vampires were thus also considered a type of revenant, and Luck ([1985] 1992:170) calls Philinnion a vampire, referring to how she preyed on the living (though not in the more familiar sense known to us through Bram Stoker's *Dracula*). W. M. S. Russell ([1980] 1981:198) suggests the phrase "solid ghost" as a synonym for "revenant." The term "zombie" is sometimes used similarly, though it originally had particular associations with voodoo, in which a dead person is allegedly restored to life by a sorcerer called a *bokor* (Guiley 1992:360). On zombies and the drugs that cause zombielike states, see Davis 1985.

20. Lawson 1964:416–17. Lawson notes that a casual allusion to the same superstition occurs also in Lucian (*Philops.* 26): " 'I know of a man,' says a doctor named Antigonus, 'who rose again twenty days after he was buried; I attended him after his resurrection as well as before his death.' 'But how was it,' rejoins another, 'that in twenty days the body did not decompose or in any case the man perish of hunger?' "

21. Lawson 1964:412 ff.

22. Granted, the part of the story that might have explained in more detail the reasons for her return is missing; we have only her statement that she returned because of "divine will."

23. Hansen 1996:66. Pausanias goes on to say that a picture of the Hero of Temesa depicted the ghost as black and wearing a wolf skin, with the name "Lycas" painted under it, while Strabo reports that the ghost was that of Polites, a companion of Odysseus who was killed by the natives through treachery. There is no mention of a rape, and the people of Temesa appease the angry ghost by collecting tribute for him. When Euthymus arrives, he defeats the Hero in a fight and forces him to release the natives from the tribute. The story also appears in Aelian (*VH* 8.18).

24. W. M. S. Russell [1980] 1981:195, referring to AT 300, "The Dragon Slayer." On this story, see also Rohde 1925:135–36; Fontenrose 1959:101–3 and 119–20; and Luck [1985] 1992:211–12.

25. Rohde 1925:134.

26. Ibid., with other examples of aggressive ghosts.

27. Plut. *Thes.* 35.5: τῶν ἐν Μαραθῶνι πρὸς Μήδους μαχομένων ἔδοξαν οὐκ ὀλίγοι φάσμα Θησέως ἐν ὅπλοις καθορᾶν πρὸ αὐτῶν ἐπὶ τοὺς βαρβάρους φερόμενον.

28. Hdt. 8.38: δύο γὰρ ὁπλίτας μέζονας ἢ κατὰ ἀνθρώπων φύσιν ἐόντας ἕπεσθαί σφι κτείνοντας καὶ διώκοντας.

29. See Rohde 1925: 136–37 for more examples.

30. The story invites comparison with the myth of Zeus and Amphitryon and the conception of Herakles.

31. The importance of water in spells and for purification is a common theme in both ancient and modern times; running water is considered particularly potent. See Halliday 1930: 126; Parker 1983: 226–27.

32. Tyrrell [1953] 1970: 44–45.

33. Spencer and Spencer 1992: 13.

34. Collison-Morley [1912] 1968: 17: "Strangely enough, we rarely find [in antiquity] any of those interesting cases, everywhere so well attested, of people appearing just about the time of their death to friends or relatives." For a detailed study of modern crisis apparitions, see Virtanen 1990.

35. On Creusa's speech, see O'Hara 1990: 88–90. Austin (1964: 289) notes the similarities between this episode and the story of another lost wife, Eurydice, in Vergil's fourth *Georgic*.

36. Apul. *Met.* 9.31: *ei per quietem obtulit sese flebilis patris sui facies, adhuc nodo revincta cervice, eique totum novercae scelus aperuit . . . et quemadmodum larvatus ad inferos demeasset.*

37. Collison-Morley [1912] 1968: 72–79.

38. Pliny 7.27.2–3: *tenuis adhuc et obscurus, obtinenti Africam comes haeserat. inclinato die spatiabatur in porticu; offertur ei mulieris figura humana grandior pulchriorque. perterrito Africam se futurorum praenuntiam dixit: iturum enim Romam honoresque gesturum, atque etiam cum summo imperio in eandem provinciam reversurum, ibique moriturum. facta sunt omnia. praeterea accedenti Carthaginem egredientique nave eadem figura in litore occurrisse narratur. ipse certe implicitus morbo futura praeteritis, adversa secundis auguratus, spem salutis nullo suorum desperante proiecit.*

39. Austin 1964: 278.

40. Dio Cass. 55.1.3: γυνὴ γάρ τις μείζων ἢ κατὰ ἀνθρώπου φύσιν ἀπαντήσασα αὐτῷ ἔφη "ποῖ δῆτα ἐπείγῃ, Δροῦσε ἀκόρεστε· οὐ πάντα σοι ταῦτα ἰδεῖν πέπρωται. ἀλλ᾽ ἄπιθι· καὶ γάρ σοι καὶ τῶν ἔργων καὶ τοῦ βίου τελευτὴ ἤδη πάρεστι."

41. Hdt. 8.84.2: φάσμα σφι γυναικὸς ἐφάνη, φανεῖσαν δὲ διακελεύσασθαι ὥστε καὶ ἅπαν ἀκοῦσαι τὸ τῶν Ἑλλήνων στρατόπεδον, ὀνειδίσασαν πρότερον τάδε· Ὦ δαιμόνιοι, μέχρι κόσου ἔτι πρύμνην ἀνακρούεσθε; It is interesting to compare the descriptions of these impressive women with Herodotus's description of Phye at 1.60.4. Pisistratus, trying to reestablish himself as tyrant at Athens, brought along Phye, "a large woman, just over six feet tall and very good-looking" (μέγαθος ἀπὸ τεσσέρων πήχεων ἀπολείπουσα τρεῖς δακτύλους καὶ ἄλλως εὐειδής). He dressed her in armor and drove into Athens, saying that the goddess Athena herself was bringing him back. The ruse was successful and Pisistratus was restored to power.

42. Plut. *Dion* 55.1.2: φάσμα γίνεται τῷ Δίωνι μέγα καὶ τερατῶδες . . . εἶδε γυναῖκα μεγάλην, στολῇ μὲν καὶ προσώπῳ μηδὲν Ἐρινύος τραγικῆς παραλλάττουσαν.

43. On the case of Brutus, cf. Shakespeare, *Julius Caesar* 4.3.274 ff., on which Collison-Morley ([1912] 1968:78) comments, "It is to Plutarch that we owe the famous story of the apparition that visited Brutus in his tent the night before the battle of Philippi, and again during the battle. Shakespeare represents it to be Caesar's ghost, but has otherwise strictly followed Plutarch."

44. Suet. *Iul.* 32: *quidam eximia magnitudine et forma in proximo sedens repente apparuit harundine canens; ad quem audiendum cum praeter pastores plurimi etiam ex stationibus milites concurrissent interque eos et aeneatores, rapta ab uno tuba prosilivit ad flumen et ingenti spiritu classicum exorsus pertendit ad alteram ripam.*

45. Hdt. 6.117.3: ἄνδρα οἱ δοκέειν ὁπλίτην ἀντιστῆναι μέγαν, τοῦ τὸ γένειον τὴν ἀσπίδα πᾶσαν σκιάζειν· τὸ δὲ φάσμα τοῦτο ἑωυτὸν μὲν παρεξελθεῖν, τὸν δὲ ἑωυτοῦ παραστάτην ἀποκτεῖναι. On this episode and other supernatural occurrences in Herodotus, see Lateiner 1990: esp. 234–40.

46. Dio Cass. 68.25: Τραιανὸς δὲ διέφυγε μὲν διὰ θυρίδος ἐκ τοῦ οἰκήματος ἐν ᾧ ἦν, προσελθόντος αὐτῷ μείζονός τινος ἢ κατὰ ἄνθρωπον καὶ ἐξαγαγόντος αὐτόν, ὥστε μικρὰ ἄττα πληγέντα περιγενέσθαι.

47. As noted in the discussion of *Met.* 9.31, if the father's ghost appeared to his daughter in a dream, it is not a true crisis apparition.

48. I thank Philip Stadter for his help with this part of the discussion.

49. Hopkins 1983:234 n. 42. See also Römer 1987.

50. Spencer and Spencer 1992:9. Poltergeist cases and their characteristics are discussed in detail in Carrington and Fodor 1951, which also includes two essays by Fodor on the psychoanalytic approach to poltergeist phenomena. See also Wilson 1981.

51. Krauss 1930:55 and 57 n. 11 list many examples of showers of stones in Livy. Krauss believes them to be solely the result of volcanic activity, but notes that there is no indication in Livy that the Romans related such showers to volcanoes, in spite of the younger Pliny's descriptions of such showers accompanying the eruption of Vesuvius (6.16–20).

52. Dodds 1973:158.

53. Suet. *Aug.* 6: *nutrimentorum eius ostenditur adhuc locus in avito suburbano iuxta Velitras permodicus et cellae penuariae instar, tenetque vicinitatem opinio tamquam et natus ibi sit. huc introire nisi necessario et caste religio est, concepta opinione veteri, quasi temere adeuntibus horror quidam et metus obiciatur, sed et mox confirmata. nam cum possessor villae novus seu forte seu temptandi causa cubitum se eo contulisset, evenit ut post paucissimas noctis horas exturbatus inde subita vi et incerta paene semianimis cum strato simul ante fores inveniretur.*

54. Dodds 1973: 158 n. 1. In this case, it is interesting to note that a young man was involved, thus providing a possible early example of an adolescent being the focus for supernatural energy.

55. See W. M. S. Russell [1980] 1981:210.

56. Dodds 1973 : 158 n. 1. For animated images, especially of metal, cf. the images animated by Hephaestus in *Iliad* 18; cf. also Talos, the bronze giant created by Hephaestus, who guarded Crete (Apollonius Rhodius 4.1637ff.). See Rose 1959 : 204 and 225 n. 84, with further references; also Bruce 1913. The "disembodied" knocking at the door in the *Mostellaria,* as we shall see, may also have depended on familiarity with poltergeist phenomena for comic effect. Though the incidents that occurred in Germanicus's room before and after his death could be classified as poltergeist phenomena, it seems to me that Tacitus here (*Ann.* 2.69.5) clearly describes witchcraft or sympathetic magic, not a poltergeist incident:

> There were found in the walls the dug-up remains of human bodies, spells, curses, lead tablets inscribed with the name of Germanicus, ashes half-buried and obscured with gore, and other evil objects that are believed to dedicate the souls to the infernal deities.

> *reperiebantur solo ac parietibus erutae humanorum corporum reliquiae, carmina et devotiones et nomen Germanici plumbeis tabulis insculptum, semusti cineres ac tabo obliti aliaque malefica quis creditur animas numinibus infernis sacrari.*

See the discussion on *defixiones* in Chapter 1, note 60.

57. Spencer and Spencer 1992 : 3 – 4, using the analogy of a tape-recording.

58. Ibid.: 5.

59. Haining 1982 : 111.

60. This local legend has raised problems for historians because the presence of horses at the battle of Marathon is not mentioned by Herodotus, our main historical source for the battle. In fact, strategists generally point out that the heavily outnumbered Athenians were able to win the battle only because the Persians did not have time to organize their cavalry. Shrimpton (1980) enumerates the various arguments for and against the presence of horses at Marathon, including the evidence from Pausanias. Further accounts of ghostly battles, including several from antiquity, can be found in Collison-Morley [1912] 1968 : 26.

61. Ameria and Tuder were in Umbria, in the north-central part of the Italian peninsula.

62. *Luc. 1.568–70: conpositis plenae gemuerunt ossibus urnae. / tum fragor armorum magnaeque per avia voces / auditae nemorum et venientes comminus umbrae.*

63. *Cim.* 1.6: ἐπὶ πολὺν δὲ χρόνον εἰδώλων τινῶν ἐν τῷ τόπῳ προφαινομένων καὶ στεναγμῶν ἐξακουομένων, ὡς οἱ πατέρες ἡμῶν λέγουσι, τὰς θύρας ἀνῳκοδόμησαν τοῦ πυριατηρίου. Bonner (1932) has observed that "in the later age of the Greek world demons were supposed to haunt baths. . . . The belief in the diabolical haunting of baths continued to exist in Egypt down to medieval and modern times" (203, 207–8). He suggests that superstitions about baths are natural outgrowths from ancient Greek beliefs about river-gods, nymphs, and nereids, who were variously friendly and

dangerous, and notes the myth about the seizure of Hylas (Theocritus 13, for example).

64. Spencer and Spencer 1992:9.

Chapter Three

1. This chapter deals with many of the similarities between ancient and modern ghost stories. Some of the changes in ghost stories over time are discussed in the last chapter of this book.

2. Dégh 1980:187.

3. Grider 1997:15.

4. Sherwin-White [1966] 1985:436. It should be noted that setting ghost stories in large, empty houses and "lonely castles" did not originate in the nineteenth century, but rather developed out of the Gothic supernatural horror novels of the eighteenth century, beginning with Horace Walpole's *The Castle of Otranto* (1764). See Chapter 7.

5. Luck [1985] 1992:187.

6. Nardi 1960:8–10.

7. Nardi, in discussing these manifestations of hauntings, never explicitly draws the distinction between recording-type ghosts and interactive ones.

8. Winkler 1980:156.

9. Ibid.: 156–57.

10. Radermacher 1979:206.

11. Nardi 1960:99.

12. Radermacher 1979:205.

13. Nardi 1960:99.

14. Jenkins [1982] 1984:168.

15. AT 326.

16. Ellis 1993.

17. Baughman 1945.

18. For the motif of the inexplicable bargain, cf. the urban legend known as the "Death Car." The story involves an expensive car (such as a Mercedes) advertised at a very low price. The buyer is overjoyed at the bargain, until discovering the car is unusable because the interior reeks, and the odor cannot be removed. Upon investigating, the new owner finds out that there had been a suicide or murder in the car, with the corpse long undiscovered, and the car now retains a lingering smell of death. See Brunvand 1981:20ff.

19. Enright 1994:2.

20. The information in this paragraph concerning North Carolina's disclosure law is taken from Goodwin 1994.

21. Sumwalt 1995.

22. Shain 1994.

23. Information about this case is taken from the *Patriot News*, Harrisburg, Pa., Oct. 27, 1996, sec. 1, p. 1.

24. Cic. *off.* 3.13.54: *vendat aedes vir bonus propter aliqua vitia, quae ipse norit, ceteri ignorent, pestilentes sint et habeantur salubres, ignoretur in omnibus cubiculis apparere serpentes, male materiatae et ruinosae, sed hoc praeter dominum nemo sciat; quaero, si haec emptoribus venditor non dixerit aedesque vendiderit pluris multo, quam se venditurum putarit, num id iniuste aut improbe fecerit.* This is a case of *reticentia* by the seller. See Dyck 1996 : 562–63.

25. W. M. S. Russell [1980] 1981 : 109.

26. Pliny does not specify whether Athenodorus made inquiries from the actual owner or realtor, or simply someone in the neighborhood not involved in the sale of the house.

27. *iterum interrogatus est, si quis timoris causa emigrasset, deberet mercedem necne. respondit, si causa fuisset, cur periculum timeret, quamvis periculum vere non fuisset, tamen non debere mercedem: sed si causa timoris iusta non fuisset, nihilo minus debere.* Mommsen 1985, 19.2.27.1. See Nardi 1960 : 63.

28. Nardi 1960 : 66–67, 178–79; Frier 1980 : 95.

29. Frier 1980 : 92.

30. Anson 1977 : 17.

31. Asimov and Pohl [1991] 1993. For other examples of ghosts and legal matters, including some real cases, see Lang 1896 : 248–73.

32. Nardi 1960 : 25. See also Dyck 1996 : 563.

Chapter Four

1. For a discussion of the date of the *Mostellaria*, see Duckworth 1952 : 56 n. 43. He cites a range of possible dates from 200 to 194 B.C. Toynbee (1971 : 34–35) points out that the *Mostellaria* is our main literary source for Roman afterlife beliefs before the first century B.C.

2. Radermacher 1979 : 206. Duckworth (1952 : 53 n. 35) is more tentative: "Plautus did not adapt the *Mostellaria* from Menander's *Phasma*, as this was later translated by Luscius Lanuvinus, and very badly, according to Terence (*Eun.* 9). If the reference to Diphilus and Philemon in *Most.* 1149 is taken over from the Greek, the author was probably Theognetus." Duckworth refers to the allusion at *Mostellaria* 1149–51, where Tranio says to Theopropides: "If you are a friend of Diphilus or Philemon, tell them how you've been ridiculed by your servants; you'll have given them the best deception scenes in all comedy" (*si amicus Diphilo aut Philemoni es, / dicito is, quo pacto tuo' te servos ludificaverit: / optumas frustrationes dederis in comoediis*). But Plautus in this passage may be asserting that he has improved upon his original, in which case the author of the *Phasma* could be Philemon. The fragmentary play by Luscius Lanuvinus entitled *Phasma* is not about a ghost. See Garton 1972.

3. Nardi (1960:99), Collart (1970:17), and Radermacher (1979:206), among others, accept this story as a traditional haunted-house legend.

4. Sturtevant 1925:82.

5. As often in Plautine comedy: see discussion in Segal 1987:27ff.

6. *Most.* 476−505:

TR. scelus, inquam, factum est iam diu, antiquom et vetus.

TH. antiquom?

TR.   id adeo nos nunc factum invenimus.

TH. quid istuc †est sceleste†? aut quis id fecit? cedo.

TR. hospes necavit hospitem captum manu;

iste, ut ego opinor, qui has tibi aedis vendidit.   480

TH. necavit?

TR.   aurumque ei ademit hospiti

eumque hic defodit hospitem ibidem in aedibus.

TH. quapropter id vos factum suspicamini?

TR. ego dicam, ausculta. ut foris cenaverat

tuo' gnatus, postquam rediit a cena domum,   485

abimus omnes cubitum; condormivimus:

lucernam forte oblitus fueram exstinguere;

atque ille exclamat derepente maxumum.

TH. quis homo? an gnatus meus?

TR.   st! tace, ausculta modo.

ait venisse illum in somnis ad se mortuom.   490

TH. nempe ergo in somnis?

TR.   ita. sed ausculta modo.

ait illum hoc pacto sibi dixisse mortuom—

TH. in somnis?

TR.   mirum quin vigilanti diceret,

qui abhinc sexaginta annis occisus foret.

interdum inepte stultus es, ★ ★ ★ ★   495

TH. taceo.

TR.   sed ecce quae illi in ★ ★

"ego transmarinus hospes sum Diapontius.

hic habito, haec mihi dedita est habitatio.

nam me Acheruntem recipere Orcus noluit,

quia praemature vita careo. per fidem   500

deceptus sum: hospes me hic necavit isque me

defodit insepultum clam [ibidem] in hisce aedibus,

scelestus, auri causa. nunc tu hinc emigra.

†scelestae hae† sunt aedes, impia est habitatio."

quae hic monstra fiunt, anno vix possum eloqui.   505

The asterisks at the end of lines 495 and 496 indicate lacunae. In 495, as Bettini notes, Schoell inserts *Theopropides,* but since Theopropides responds *taceo,* Bettini believes that it would be preferable to insert the fairly standard formula *quin tu taces,* citing *Curc.* 84 and *Men.* 561. He also suggests *non tu taces?* citing

Bacch. 470. Terzaghi inserts *tace modo.* At 496, Bettini agrees with Schoell's insertion of *somnis mortuos.*

7. Ziegler 1982:14.

8. Ibid.: 26.

9. *Hec.* 25–30:

> κτείνει με χρυσοῦ τὸν ταλαίπωρον χάριν
> ξένος πατρῷος καὶ κτανὼν ἐς οἶδμ' ἁλὸς
> μεθῆχ', ἵν' αὐτὸς χρυσὸν ἐν δόμοις ἔχῃ.
> κεῖμαι δ' ἐπ' ἀκταῖς, ἄλλοτ' ἐν πόντου σάλῳ,
> πολλοῖς διαύλοις κυμάτων φορούμενος,
> ἄκλαυστος, ἄταφος.

10. A later adaptation of the Polydorus story can be found in Vergil *Aen.* 3.41 ff. Of the murder, Vergil has Aeneas comment, "He killed Polydorus, and took his gold by force" (*Polydorum obtruncat, et auro / vi potitur,* 3.55–56), similar to the story of Diapontius. To lay the spirit of Polydorus to rest, Aeneas and his men hold elaborate funeral rites after the region is described as *scelerata* ("cursed" or "polluted by crime") and *pollutum hospitium* ("defiled hospitality" or "profaned guest-friendship," 3.60–61), terms also used by Tranio. Although the spirit of Polydorus did not specifically request proper burial, Aeneas knew it was the proper and necessary thing to do. The ghost invented by Tranio also does not request proper burial from Philolaches, and Tranio doesn't suggest the idea to clear the house of the spirit—that would defeat his purpose of keeping Theopropides out of the house, as discussed below.

11. It should be noted that *defodit* means simply buried or placed under the earth, but the *insepultum* indicates burial without the proper rituals. Some texts put a space, *in sepultum,* which does not convey the distinction as well.

12. It is unclear whether Plautus (and consequently Tranio) invented the proper name "Diapontius" to fit in with the story of the merchant traveling overseas, or whether Plautus inherited the name from his Greek model and then glossed it with "transmarinus." Whatever its origin, the use of wordplay here adds to the impression that Tranio is making up the story and its characters as he goes along.

13. Warmington (1961:237) says, "The story resembles the latter part of Euripides' Ἑκάβη, but the model of the play is unknown . . . the action of the play probably begins at a point where Deiphilus is dead, but Iliona is unaware of the fact." Of Ennius's *Hecuba,* only fifteen verses are left, and two words remain of the speech that may have been delivered by the ghost of Polydorus, possibly in the prologue as in Euripides: *undantem salum* ("the surging sea"), which may parallel οἶδμ' ἁλὸς (Hickman 1938:72).

14. *mater, te appello, tu quae curam somno suspenso levas / neque te mei miseret, surge et sepeli natum . . . neu reliquias quaeso meas sieris denudatis ossibus per terram sanie delibutas foede divexarier* (Warmington 1961:238–40). Beare (1950:70) calls

this "the most famous scene in Roman tragedy." Horace (*Sat.* 2.3.60–62) tells of an occasion when the actor playing Iliona really did fall asleep: "Once, when Fufius was drunk and sleeping through Iliona's cue, twelve hundred Catieni shouted, 'Mother, I'm calling you!'" (*Fufius ebrius olim, / cum Ilionam edormit, Catienis mille ducentis / "mater, te appello!" clamantibus*).

15. Hickman 1938:83.

16. Ziegler 1982:26.

17. See Fenton 1921:11 ff.; Collart 1970:105.

18. Ziegler 1982:26.

19. Ibid.:18.

20. Duckworth 1952:352.

21. Ziegler 1982:19.

22. Lawson 1964:505; and see discussion in Chapter 1.

23. Also noted by Nardi (1960:99).

24. For an extended discussion of both fictional and actual dreams in the plays of Plautus, see Ziegler 1982.

25. Suet. *Cal.* 59; Paus. 6.6.7–11. There are a few cases of haunted sites in which no effort is made to clear the site, such as Plut. *Cim.* 1.6.

26. The few cases in which dream-ghosts could be said to be "haunting" people were regularly attributed to mental instability, as we have seen in the cases of Nero, Otho, and Caracalla.

27. Sonnenschein (1907:108) believes *nempe* is used for clarification, i.e., "It was in sleep then, if I understand you?" Morris ([1880] 1881:10) observes that *nempe* was often used to clarify what had been said, "but often, as here [used] ironically, to express the contrary sense and cast doubt upon a previous statement." Cf. Ussing 1972:129.

28. Sonnenschein (1907:108) suggests that Tranio's use of *ille* in the previous line was vague, as Tranio had not quite made up his mind who shouted out, and refuses to commit himself when asked. F. R. Merrill (1972:488) agrees: "Tranio hasn't made up his mind yet who the 'ille' is to be, as we see when he avoids Theopropides' direct question in the following line. The word order of 484–488 makes it clear that Tranio is improvising as he goes along." Cf. Collart 1970:105 n. 488.

29. See discussion in Chapter 1.

30. See Pasquali 1929:314–16; Banti 1930:69 ff.; Perna 1955:370 n. 2.

31. Ziegler 1982:23–34.

32. Wieand 1920:112–13.

33. Radermacher 1979:106.

34. On the implications of *emigra,* see Chapter 3.

35. I thank George Houston for bringing this detail to my attention. The problem is also alluded to by Terzaghi (1929:99). Tranio does use *anno* indefinitely in line 505.

36. Ziegler 1982:22. *Comoedia palliata* are "comedies in Greek dress,"

that is, Roman comedies adapted from Greek predecessors. On comic door-knocking scenes, see also Brown 1995, though Brown focuses on Terence and Menander rather than on Plautus.

37. *Most.* 463–65:

TR. *occidisti hercle—*
TH.   *quem mortalem?*
TR.   *omnis tuos.*
TH. *di te deaeque omnes faxint cum istoc omine—*
TR. *metuo te atque istos expiare ut possies.*

38. Gulick 1896:236.

39. *Most.* 510: *perii! illisce hodie hanc conturbabunt fabulam.*

40. It is from the *monstra* that this play takes its title: *Mostellaria* (sc. *fabula*) is derived from *mostellum,* the diminutive of *monstrum.* The title of the play is more properly translated facetiously as "A Little Ghost Story" rather than the popular "The Haunted House."

41. See also Sutton 1993:74. There are practical considerations involved in the control over the door as well. Ziegler explains that control of stage blocking is a sign that Tranio has Theopropides right where he wants him—both literally and figuratively (1982:22–23).

42. Duckworth (1952:220–21) discusses the foreshadowing. See also Wieand 1920:111.

43. *Most.* 389–90: *satin habes si ego advenientem ita patrem faciam tuom, / non modo ne intro eat, verum etiam ut fugiat longe ab aedibus? Most.* 423–24: *facturum ⟨me⟩ ut ne etiam aspicere aedis audeat, / capite obvoluto ut fugiat cum summo metu.*

44. Wieand 1920:113; also Banti 1930:67.

45. Sutton 1993:76.

46. See also Duckworth 1952:245. Sutton (1993:73) notes that Tranio's "complicated and fantastic" story manages to play on Theopropides' "superstitious side." The name Theopropides ("Son of Prophecy") is ironic. Duckworth (348) points out two other instances in Plautus of ironical names grafted onto *senes* deceived by their slaves: Nicobulus ("Conquering in Counsel") from the *Bacchides* and Periphanes ("Notable") from the *Epidicus.*

47. Jebb 1909:143.

48. Halliday 1930:131.

Chapter Five

1. For information on Sura, see Syme 1958, app. 85 and index; also Sherwin-White [1966] 1985:309–11. Pliny addresses letter 4.30 to Sura as well. Sura, a soldier, orator, and right-hand man to the emperor Trajan, was also a patron of the arts whose clients included the poet Martial (see Martial 6.64.12–13 and 7.47.1–2). Little is known about Sura's family.

2. Pliny 7.27.1: *perquam velim scire, esse phantasmata et habere propriam figuram numenque aliquod putes an inania et vana ex metu nostro imaginem accipere.*

3. Other letters Pliny structures around three examples include 2.20 (on his unscrupulous contemporary Regulus) and 3.16 (on the virtue of Arria). See Kenney and Clausen 1982: 160 ff., with further references.

4. Pliny 7.27.12–14: *est libertus mihi non inlitteratus. cum hoc minor frater eodem lecto quiescebat. is visus est sibi cernere quendam in toro residentem admoventemque capiti suo cultros, atque etiam ex ipso vertice amputantem capillos. ubi inluxit, ipse circa verticem tonsus, capilli iacentes reperiuntur. exiguum temporis medium, et rursus simile aliud priori fidem fecit. puer in paedagogio mixtus pluribus dormiebat. venerunt per fenestras (ita narrat) in tunicis albis duo cubantemque detonderunt et qua venerant recesserunt. hunc quoque tonsum sparsosque circa capillos dies ostendit. nihil notabile secutum, nisi forte quod non fui reus, futurus, si Domitianus sub quo haec acciderunt, diutius vixisset. nam in scrinio eius datus a Caro de me libellus inventus est; ex quo coniectari potest, quia reis moris est summittere capillum, recisos meorum capillos depulsi quod imminebat periculi signum fuisse.*

5. Sherwin-White [1966] 1985: 437.

6. W. M. S. Russell [1980] 1981: 204.

7. Merrill [1903] 1911: 362; Sherwin-White [1966] 1985: 437.

8. Merrill [1903] 1911: 362.

9. For example, Apul. *Met.* 4.27: "Night visions often do foretell opposite outcomes" (*nocturnae visiones contrarios eventus nonnumquam pronuntiant*). The old woman who says this, however, is a suspicious character.

10. Pliny never gives Domitian his titles, observing the *damnatio memoriae* in the letters. So the Caesar referred to here should be Titus. Additionally, there is very little hint here of the terror induced by Domitian, and the case could be the *iudicium quadruplex* mentioned as a case of his youth in 4.24.1. But a date in the early years of Domitian's reign is possible. See Sherwin-White [1966] 1985: 128.

11. Pliny is quoting from *Iliad* 12.243.

12. Pliny 1.18.2–4: *refert tamen, eventura soleas an contraria somniare. mihi reputanti somnium meum istud, quod times tu, egregiam actionem portendere videtur. susceperam causam Iuni Pastoris, cum mihi quiescenti visa est socrus mea advoluta genibus ne agerem obsecrare; et eram acturus adulescentulus adhuc, eram in quadruplici iudicio, eram contra potentissimos civitatis atque etiam Caesaris amicos, quae singula excutere mentem mihi post tam triste somnium poterant. egi tamen* λογισάμενος *illud* εἰς οἰωνὸς ἄριστος ἀμύνεσθαι περὶ πάτρης. *nam mihi patria, et si quid carius patria, fides videbatur. prospere cessit, atque adeo illa actio mihi aures hominum, illa ianuam famae patefecit.*

13. The mother-in-law in question was most likely Pompeia Celerina, also mentioned in letter 1.4. She was the mother of Pliny's first (or possibly second) wife, not of Calpurnia, his second (or possibly third) wife. For the controversy over the number of Pliny's marriages, see Sherwin-White [1966] 1985: 559

and Syme 1958:84, where Pompeia Celerina is listed as the mother of Pliny's second wife. In letter 4.19 Pliny describes to Hispulla, the aunt of his wife Calpurnia, how interested Calpurnia is in Pliny's work, his affection for her, and the gratitude he feels toward Hispulla as the cause of their mutual happiness. Hispulla, the aunt, had raised Calpurnia, which indicates that Calpurnia's mother and father were most likely deceased early on. So Pompeia Celerina, named as *socrus* ("mother-in-law") in letter 1.4, would have been the mother not of Calpurnia, but of an earlier wife of Pliny (Prichard and Bernard 1896: 12, 37–38). Pliny himself was a young man at the time of the dream he describes here, and probably still married to his first wife, so Pompeia Celerina was most likely already dead, and it is her ghost that appears in his dream. The incident would have been less remarkable and less disturbing otherwise, and Pliny might have mentioned whether his mother-in-law had expressed this concern over his lawsuit while he was awake.

14. This would not, however, be the first recorded instance in antiquity of tokens being left behind to prove the reality of an apparition. In Pindar *Olympian* 13.61.80, Athena leaves a bridle for an incubated sleeper. See Van Lieshout 1980:21–23, for more examples. The cutting of hair was also associated with mourning: Achilles cuts off a long lock of hair and places it on Patroclus's bier, and Orestes leaves a lock of hair on his father's tomb. Burkert (1985:70) points out that hair offerings were also common at sanctuaries.

15. This was done then, as now, by putting up a notice (*titulus*) in front of the house (Prichard and Bernard 1896:49).

16. Pliny 7.27.5–11: *erat Athenis spatiosa et capax domus sed infamis et pestilens. per silentium noctis sonus ferri, et si attenderes acrius, strepitus vinculorum longius primo, deinde e proximo reddebatur: mox adparebat idolon, senex macie et squalore confectus, promissa barba, horrenti capillo; cruribus compedes, manibus catenas gerebat quatiebatque. inde inhabitantibus tristes diraeque noctes per metum vigilabantur; vigiliam morbus et crescente formidine mors sequebatur. nam interdiu quoque, quamquam abscesserat imago, memoria imaginis oculis inerrabat, longiorque causis timoris timor erat. deserta inde et damnata solitudine domus totaque illi monstro relicta; proscribebatur tamen, seu quis emere seu quis conducere ignarus tanti mali vellet. venit Athenas philosophus Athenodorus, legit titulum auditoque pretio, quia suspecta vilitas, percunctatus omnia docetur ac nihilo minus, immo tanto magis conducit. ubi coepit advesperascere, iubet sterni sibi in prima domus parte, poscit pugillares stilum lumen, suos omnes in interiora dimittit; ipse ad scribendum animum oculos manum intendit, ne vacua mens audita simulacra et inanes sibi metus fingeret. initio, quale ubique, silentium noctis; dein concuti ferrum, vincula moveri. ille non tollere oculos, non remittere stilum, sed offirmare animum auribusque praetendere. tum crebrescere fragor, adventare et iam ut in limine, iam ut intra limen audiri. respicit, videt agnoscitque narratam sibi effigiem. stabat innuebatque digito similis vocanti. hic contra ut paulum exspectaret manu significat rursusque ceris et stilo incumbit. illa scribentis capiti catenis insonabat. respicit rursus idem quod prius innuentem, nec moratus tollit lumen et sequitur. ibat illa lento gradu quasi gravis vinculis.*

postquam deflexit in aream domus, repente dilapsa deserit comitem. desertus herbas et folia concerpta signum loco ponit. postero die adit magistratus, monet ut illum locum effodi iubeant. inveniuntur ossa inserta catenis et implicita, quae corpus aevo terraque putrefactum nuda et exesa reliquerat vinculis; collecta publice sepeliuntur. domus postea rite conditis manibus caruit.

17. Schwartz 1969:673.

18. Cic. *Fin.* 5.1.1: *is locus ab omni turba id temporis vacuus esset . . . cum autem venissemus in Academiae non sine causa nobilitata spatia, solitudo erat ea quam volueramus.* Schwartz 1969:673.

19. Tarsus, in Asia Minor, was the seat of a philosophical school that produced many Stoics. The school was especially active in the first century B.C.

20. Merrill [1903] 1911:360; Schwartz 1969:671–72.

21. Schwartz 1969:672. But the Academy, which was full of Skeptics, would probably not have extended a warm welcome to a Stoic, and it seems unlikely that a Stoic philosopher would have wanted to rent a house in a part of town swarming with Skeptics.

22. Nardi 1960:111.

23. Schwartz (1969:675) cites this and another passage from the Midrash.

24. King David was destined to die on the Sabbath. He did not want to die on that day, because on the Sabbath no one could bury him. God decreed that if David read the Torah incessantly, the Angel of Death could not harm him:

> King David spent the entire Sabbath day in devoted study of the Torah. And, when the Sabbath on which he was to die arrived, the Angel of Death rose up against him; but he had no power over him, for King David did not cease his studying. "What shall I do with him?" cried the Angel of Death in exasperation. Behind the royal palace lay a lovely garden, and so the Angel of Death entered it and began to shake the trees. Hearing the noise, David went to see who was disturbing the Sabbath peace. And as he walked he did not cease his devoted study of the Torah. But as he descended the steps he lost his balance and for one instant the sacred words became stilled on his lips. In that very instant the Angel of Death smote him.

Because no one was allowed to bury David, his son Solomon lamented, "A live dog is better than a dead lion" (Ausubel [1948] 1977:477).

25. See MacKenzie 1971:82 for examples.

26. Römer 1987:30.

27. Here Sherwin-White ([1966] 1985:437) comments, "Pliny gets this point right. The burial of an unknown man could only be done by the representative of the community, who would also be concerned at the improper burial of a corpse within the city precinct or its removal." He cites the *lex coloniae Genitivae Iuliae seu Ursonensis* from Abbot and Johnson 1926:303 no. 26. But this municipal document applied to towns with colonial status in Italy and in the provinces (Urso was in Spain), and Pliny's story is set in Athens, which was not a *colonia*. This is an instance of conflation in the story: although the

setting is Greek, Athenodorus follows Roman procedure. As we shall see, in Lucian's version of this legend, set in Corinth, the philosopher informs not the magistrate but the owner of the house. Anyway, it's unlikely that the intended audience of this story would have cared which procedure was followed.

28. Nardi 1960:99; Lawson 1964:505.

29. Lilja 1978:58.

30. Schwartz 1969:675–76. For an extended discussion of physical representations of philosophers of different schools, see Zanker 1995:257 and 260–62. The ghost of the old man in Pliny's story seems to fit the description of the long-haired Charismatics or the Pythagoreans, who affected a similar image. Cf. also Vergil's description of Hector's ghost with a "filthy beard" (*squalentem barbam, Aen.* 2.277).

31. Pliny does not use *spectrum, species, larva, umbra,* or *facies,* though these words occur frequently in other supernatural literature of the time, such as Apuleius's *Metamorphoses.*

32. As noted in Chapter 3, if the inhabitants left right away, there wouldn't be much of a story. Often an explanation may be given, such as that the inhabitants had made a large investment and did not feel that they could simply abandon the house.

33. Cic. *Fin.* 5.1.2: *venit enim mihi Platonis in mentem, quem accepimus primum hic disputare solitum; cuius etiam illi propinqui hortuli non memoriam solum mihi afferunt sed ipsum videntur in conspectu meo ponere.*

34. Having the ghost speak would detract from the mysterious atmosphere that Pliny has so successfully created. The ghost's lack of oral communication may also be connected with the idea that ghosts could not speak until spoken to, though in this story Athenodorus does not even try to address the ghost.

35. See discussion in Chapter 1, with examples from Lucian *Philops.* 15, Paus. 9.38.5, and the tenth Declamation ascribed to Quintilian; also Rohde 1925:52 n. 72; Fontenrose [1978] 1981:130; Faraone 1991b; and Larson 1995:134.

36. Pliny 5.5.5–7: *Gaius quidem Fannius, quod accidit, multo ante praesensit. visus est sibi per nocturnam quietem iacere in lectulo suo compositus in habitum studentis, habere ante se scrinium (ita solebat); mox imaginatus est venisse Neronem, in toro resedisse, prompsisse primum librum quem de sceleribus eius ediderat, eumque ad extremum revolvisse; idem in secundo ac tertio fecisse, tunc abisse. expavit et sic interpretatus est, tamquam idem sibi futurus esset scribendi finis, qui fuisset illi legendi: et fuit idem.*

37. Note also the use of similar phrases in other ghost stories discussed in previous chapters: *ea nocte per quietem* (Suet. *Otho* 7); *per quietem* (Apul. *Met.* 9.31).

38. Pliny uses *compositus* elsewhere only with the meaning "settled," e.g., "the villa . . . in which the man had settled so happily" (*villa . . . in qua se composuerat homo felicior,* 5.18.1). But other writers of the first century A.D. did use it to mean "laid out in the attitude of death" (*composita in mortem iacuit,*

Lucan 9.116, on Pompey's wife Cornelia, in her grief). Persius, too, describes a dead man "laid out on his bed" (*compositus lecto, 3.105*).

39. Drusus Nero was the brother of Tiberius and stepson of the emperor Augustus, who considered him his best general and entrusted him with the invasion of Germany. Drusus made four successive attacks in Germany from 12 to 9 B.C., with a string of victories. But he died at age 29 from an illness he contracted after a bad fall from his horse.

40. Pliny 3.5.4: *"Bellorum Germaniae viginti"; quibus omnia quae cum Germanis gessimus bella collegit. incohavit cum in Germania militaret, somnio monitus: adstitit ei quiescenti Drusi Neronis effigies, qui Germaniae latissime victor ibi periit, commendabat memoriam suam orabatque ut se ab iniuria oblivionis adsereret.*

41. Rather ironic when we consider Nero's own nightmares about Agrippina (Suet. *Ner.* 34).

42. Pliny 7.27.16: *licet etiam utramque in partem (ut soles) disputes, ex altera tamen fortius, ne me suspensum incertumque dimittas, cum mihi consulendi causa fuerit, ut dubitare desinerem.*

Chapter Six

1. Lucian wrote approximately eighty pieces, most in dialogue form, satirizing a variety of topics such as popular religion, ethnographic writing, and philosophic pretension.

2. *Philops.* 1: Ἔχεις μοι, ὦ Φιλόκλεις, εἰπεῖν τί ποτε ἄρα ἐστὶν ὃ πολλοὺς εἰς ἐπιθυμίαν τοῦ ψεύδεσθαι προάγεται, ὡς αὐτούς τε χαίρειν μηδὲν ὑγιὲς λέγοντας καὶ τοῖς τὰ τοιαῦτα διεξιοῦσιν μάλιστα προσέχειν τὸν νοῦν...

3. *Philops.* 2. Lucian is referring to Herodotus 6.105–6.

4. C. P. Jones 1986:47.

5. Ibid.: 48.

6. Jones (ibid.) calls this the most famous story in the dialogue. See AT 325, "Apprentice and Ghost"; and Christiansen 1958:28 ff., type 3020, "Inexperienced Use of the Black Book."

7. *Philops.* 27: ὁ Εὐκράτης ὥσπερ ἀναμνησθεὶς πρὸς τὴν ὄψιν τῶν υἱέων, Οὕτως ὀναίμην, ἔφη, τούτων—ἐπιβαλὼν αὐτοῖς τὴν χεῖρα— ἀληθῆ, ὦ Τυχιάδη, πρός σε ἐρῶ. τὴν μακαρῖτίν μου γυναῖκα τὴν τούτων μητέρα πάντες ἴσασιν ὅπως ἠγάπησα, ἐδήλωσα δὲ οἷς περὶ αὐτὴν ἔπραξα οὐ ζῶσαν μόνον, ἀλλὰ καὶ ἐπεὶ ἀπέθανεν, τόν τε κόσμον ἅπαντα συγκατακαύσας καὶ τὴν ἐσθῆτα ᾗ ζῶσα ἔχαιρεν. ἑβδόμη δὲ μετὰ τὴν τελευτὴν ἡμέρᾳ ἐγὼ μὲν ἐνταῦθα ἐπὶ τῆς κλίνης ὥσπερ νῦν ἐκείμην παραμυθούμενος τὸ πένθος· ἀνεγίνωσκον γὰρ τὸ περὶ ψυχῆς τοῦ Πλάτωνος βιβλίον ἐφ' ἡσυχίας· ἐπεισέρχεται δὲ μεταξὺ ἡ Δημαινέτη αὐτὴ ἐκείνη καὶ καθίζεται πλησίον ὥσπερ νῦν Εὐκρατίδης οὑτοσί—δείξας τὸν νεώτερον τῶν υἱέων· ὁ δὲ αὐτίκα ἔφριξε μάλα

παιδικῶς, καὶ πάλαι ἤδη ὠχρὸς ὢν πρὸς τὴν διήγησιν—Ἐγὼ δέ, ἦ δ'
ὃς ὁ Εὐκράτης, ὡς εἶδον, περιπλακεὶς αὐτῇ ἐδάκρυον ἀνακωκύσας· ἡ
δὲ οὐκ εἴα βοᾶν, ἀλλ' ᾐτιᾶτό με ὅτι τὰ ἄλλα πάντα χαρισάμενος αὐτῇ
θάτερον τοῖν σανδάλοιν χρυσοῖν ὄντοιν οὐ κατακαύσαιμι, εἶναι δὲ
αὐτὸ ἔφασκεν παραπεσὸν ὑπὸ τῇ κιβωτῷ. καὶ διὰ τοῦτο ἡμεῖς οὐχ
εὑρόντες θάτερον μόνον ἐκαύσαμεν. ἔτι δὲ ἡμῶν διαλεγομένων κατά-
ρατόν τι κυνίδιον ὑπὸ τῇ κλίνῃ ὂν Μελιταῖον ὑλάκτησεν, ἡ δὲ ἠφανίσθη
πρὸς τὴν ὑλακήν. τὸ μέντοι σανδάλιον εὑρέθη ὑπὸ τῇ κιβωτῷ καὶ κα-
τεκαύθη ὕστερον.

8. Anderson 1976a:25–27; C. P. Jones 1986:50.

9. G. Anderson 1976a:24–27. He also mentions the possibility that Lucian was drawing on collections such as a περὶ θαυμασίων ("On Marvels"),
but does not pursue it.

10. In doing so, Demainete is also less sympathetic than other, more tragic
figures who complain of improper burial, such as Patroclus and Polydorus.

11. Edmunds 1984. Initiates headed to the Eleusinian mysteries, for example, wore only one sandal. Cf. the film "Monty Python's Life of Brian," in
which the unwilling messiah Brian accidentally loses a sandal, prompting his
zealous cult followers to take up the cry, "Follow the Sandal!" and to go with
only one foot shod, in hopes of reaching a higher spiritual plane.

12. The Maltese had evidently been one of the most popular domestic
dogs for centuries, as many representations of it appear on Attic vases and
gravestones from the fifth century B.C. Publius's dog Issa was probably a Maltese (Mart. 1.109). See Toynbee 1948.

13. See discussion in Chapter 1. Lucian's dialogue has an urban rather than
a rural setting, another possible reason for the difference in the breed of dog.

14. G. Anderson 1976a:28.

15. C. P. Jones 1986:50.

16. Radermacher 1979:206–7. Jones (1986:50) does believe that most of
Lucian's stories came from oral sources. But he specifically cites the two ghost
stories as examples of how "some of Lucian's inventions are inspired by literature," and gives the specific references from Herodotus and Pliny.

17. *Philops.* 29: τουτονὶ τὸν ἀδαμάντινον πείθομεν . . . ἡγεῖσθαι δαί-
μονάς τινας εἶναι καὶ φάσματα καὶ νεκρῶν ψυχὰς περιπολεῖν ὑπὲρ γῆς
καὶ φαίνεσθαι οἷς ἂν ἐθέλωσιν.

18. *Philops.* 29: Μὰ Δί' . . . ἀλλ' οὐδὲ ὅλως εἶναι τὰ τοιαῦτα . . . οἴεται.

19. *Philops.* 30–31: Ἀλλά, ἦ δ' ὅς, ἤν ποτε εἰς Κόρινθον ἔλθῃς, ἐροῦ
ἔνθα ἐστὶν ἡ Εὐβατίδου οἰκία, καὶ ἐπειδάν σοι δειχθῇ παρὰ τὸ Κρά-
νειον, παρελθὼν εἰς αὐτὴν λέγε πρὸς τὸν θυρωρὸν Τίβειον ὡς ἐθέλοις
ἰδεῖν ὅθεν τὸν δαίμονα ὁ Πυθαγορικὸς Ἀρίγνωτος ἀνορύξας ἀπήλασε
καὶ πρὸς τὸ λοιπὸν οἰκεῖσθαι τὴν οἰκίαν ἐποίησεν.

Τί δὲ τοῦτο ἦν, ὦ Ἀρίγνωτε; ἤρετο ὁ Εὐκράτης. Ἀοίκητος ἦν, ἦ δ' ὅς,
ἐκ πολλοῦ ὑπὸ δειμάτων, εἰ δέ τις οἰκήσειεν εὐθὺς ἐκπλαγεὶς ἔφευγεν,

ἐκδιωχθεὶς ὑπό τινος φοβεροῦ καὶ ταραχώδους φάσματος. συνέπιπτεν οὖν ἤδη καὶ ἡ στέγη κατέρρει, καὶ ὅλως οὐδεὶς ἦν ὁ θαρρήσων παρελθεῖν ἐς αὐτήν.

Ἐγὼ δὲ ἐπεὶ ταῦτα ἤκουσα, τὰς βίβλους λαβὼν—εἰσὶν δέ μοι Αἰγύπτιαι μάλα πολλαὶ περὶ τῶν τοιούτων—ἧκον ἐς τὴν οἰκίαν περὶ πρῶτον ὕπνον ἀποτρέποντος τοῦ ξένου καὶ μόνον οὐκ ἐπιλαμβανομένου, ἐπεὶ ἔμαθεν οἷ βαδίζοιμι, εἰς προὖπτον κακόν, ὡς ᾤετο. ἐγὼ δὲ λύχνον λαβὼν μόνος εἰσέρχομαι, καὶ ἐν τῷ μεγίστῳ οἰκήματι καταθεὶς τὸ φῶς ἀνεγίνωσκον ἡσυχῇ χαμαὶ καθεζόμενος· ἐφίσταται δὲ ὁ δαίμων ἐπί τινα τῶν πολλῶν ἥκειν νομίζων καὶ δεδίξεσθαι κἀμὲ ἐλπίζων ὥσπερ τοὺς ἄλλους, αὐχμηρὸς καὶ κομήτης καὶ μελάντερος τοῦ ζόφου. καὶ ὁ μὲν ἐπιστὰς ἐπειρᾶτό μου, πανταχόθεν προσβάλλων εἴ ποθεν κρατήσειεν, καὶ ἄρτι μὲν κύων ἄρτι δὲ ταῦρος γιγνόμενος ἢ λέων. ἐγὼ δὲ προχειρισάμενος τὴν φρικωδεστάτην ἐπίρρησιν αἰγυπτιάζων τῇ φωνῇ συνήλασα κατάδων αὐτὸν εἴς τινα γωνίαν σκοτεινοῦ οἰκήματος· ἰδὼν δὲ αὐτὸν οἷ κατέδυ, τὸ λοιπὸν ἀνεπαυόμην.

Ἕωθεν δὲ πάντων ἀπεγνωκότων καὶ νεκρὸν εὑρήσειν με οἰομένων καθάπερ τοὺς ἄλλους, προελθὼν ἀπροσδόκητος ἅπασι πρόσειμι τῷ Εὐβατίδῃ, εὐαγγελιζόμενος αὐτῷ ὅτι καθαρὰν αὐτοῦ καὶ ἀδείμαντον ἤδη ἕξει τὴν οἰκίαν οἰκεῖν. παραλαβὼν οὖν αὐτόν τε καὶ τῶν ἄλλων πολλούς—εἵποντο γὰρ τοῦ παραδόξου ἕνεκα—ἐκέλευον ἀγαγὼν ἐπὶ τὸν τόπον οὗ καταδεδυκότα τὸν δαίμονα ἑωράκειν, σκάπτειν λαβόντας δικέλλας καὶ σκαφεῖα, καὶ ἐπειδὴ ἐποίησαν, εὑρέθη ὅσον ἐπ᾽ ὄργυιαν κατορωρυγμένος τις νεκρὸς ἕωλος μόνα τὰ ὀστᾶ κατὰ σχῆμα συγκείμενος. ἐκεῖνον μὲν οὖν ἐθάψαμεν ἀνορύξαντες, ἡ οἰκία δὲ τὸ ἀπ᾽ ἐκείνου ἐπαύσατο ἐνοχλουμένη ὑπὸ τῶν φασμάτων.

20. Adapted from Nardi 1960:111.

21. Ibid.

22. *Philops.* 29: κἀγὼ μὲν ὡς εἶδον αὐτὸν ἀνέπνευσα, τοῦτ᾽ ἐκεῖνο ἥκειν μοι νομίσας πέλεκύν τινα κατὰ τῶν ψευσμάτων. Ἐπιστομιεῖ γὰρ αὐτούς, ἔλεγον, ὁ σοφὸς ἀνὴρ οὕτω τεράστια διεξιόντας.

23. G. Anderson 1976a:28. *Magus gloriosus,* "The Boastful Magician," is a play on *miles gloriosus,* "The Braggart Soldier," a stock character in comedy.

24. Nardi 1960:112.

25. See discussion in Chapter 1.

26. G. Anderson 1976a:28.

27. See Chapter 1 and Rohde 1925:134 ff.

28. Apollodorus 3.13.5; Ovid *Met.* 11.217 and 400 ff. Many sea deities could change their shapes.

29. *Od.* 4.363–570.

30. The Molossian was a mastiff-like breed used mainly as a sheepdog or a watchdog. See Toynbee 1948.

31. Johnston 1995:363–64, adding that shape-shifting "is liminal insofar as it is hybrid." See also Winkler 1980:161 n. 23.

    32. Brown 1979:74–77.

    33. Vermeule 1979:8. For example, Pliny the Elder records how the soul of Aristeas at Proconnesus was seen flying out of his mouth in the shape of a raven (*HN* 52.174–75). Probably the most well-known modern example of a bird with ghostly or daimonic qualities can be found in Edgar Allan Poe's "The Raven" (1845), as in the last stanza (lines 103–8):

> And the Raven, never flitting, still is sitting, *still* is sitting
> On the pallid bust of Pallas just above my chamber door;
> And his eyes have all the seeming of a demon's that is dreaming,
> And the lamp-light o'er him streaming throws his shadow on the floor;
> And my soul from out that shadow that lies floating on the floor
>   Shall be lifted—nevermore!

The raven in this poem has been frequently interpreted as representing the desolate narrator's inclination to self-torment and inability to move beyond his grief at the death of "the lost Lenore" (line 10). For the text, with notes, see Mabbot 1969:364–74; for criticism and further references, see Frank and Magistrale 1997:300–301.

    34. Brown 1979:74–77.

    35. See Winkler 1980:161 n. 23.

    36. Finucane 1982:20.

    37. Cumont [1922] 1923:67.

    38. C. P. Jones 1986:51.

    39. Ibid.: 4.

    40. Ibid.: 26–29.

    41. Ibid.: 51. Another Platonist of the same epoch is Apuleius, who was accused of using the black arts himself, and whose *Metamorphoses* contain incidents of magic and the supernatural that are similar to the ones described in Lucian. The witches in *Met.* 2.22, for example, "change themselves into birds, then dogs and mice, and indeed even flies" (*nam et aves et rursum canes et mures, immo vero etiam muscas, induunt*), though not necessarily in quick succession, as the ghost does in Lucian's story. See also Scobie 1978; Johnston 1995:374 n. 32.

    42. G. Anderson 1976a:28.

Chapter Seven

    1. Haining 1982:155. That is, Lucian's is the earliest *surviving* account of such a group of tale-tellers.

    2. Shelley 1965:viii–ix.

    3. H. James 1992:115.

    4. Machen [1948] 1973:73–76. This story, written in 1914, also reflects the popularity of ghostly armies.

    5. See Olrik [1921] 1992:33–34.

    6. Palmer 1988:298.

7. Ibid.: 297. There is a good entry on the "Angel of Mons" problem in Guiley 1992:11.

8. M. R. James 1987:57–77. For a good study of M. R. James's life, career, and antiquarian interests, see Pfaff 1980.

9. *Iste,* a demonstrative pronoun of the second person, originally meant "that (of yours)." It eventually acquired a contemptuous character, from the refusal to take any direct notice of the person under discussion, "the person *at* whom one speaks or points" (Gildersleeve and Lodge [1867] 1986:192, ¶306). In this story, *iste* suggests that the person referred to in the inscription is someone extremely unpleasant.

10. L. C. Jones 1959:39, 58.

11. Hearn 1976:73.

12. Ibid.: 73–74. Commenting on the flame, Hearn cites the folk-belief that a candle will burn dim or blue in the presence of an apparition, and suggests that Dickens possibly knew this superstition from Shakespeare: Brutus observes at the appearance of Caesar's ghost, "How ill this taper burns!" (*Julius Caesar* 4.3.275). But, as we have seen, Shakespeare himself seems likely to have derived this description from Plutarch, who describes Brutus's tent as dimly lit. Shakespeare's source for Plutarch was Sir Thomas North, *The Lives of the Noble Grecians and Romans* (1579), which North himself had translated, not from the original Greek, but from the French version of Jacques Amyot (1559). See Dorsch [1955] 1983:xii.

13. Hearn 1976:74.

14. Ibid.: 77.

15. Ibid.: 76.

16. This passage and the ones following are from Wilde 1906:21–24, and 104.

17. See Sarkissian 1985 for an extended discussion of humor in "The Canterville Ghost."

18. L. C. Jones 1959:59.

19. Nardi 1960:10; Rust 1988:443.

20. See Daly 1990.

21. Krauss 1930:158.

22. Suet. *Ner.* 46.2. The emperor Vespasian, on the other hand, was not inclined to take such portents particularly seriously: "Not even in times of dread or in danger of death did Vespasian refrain from joking. For when, among other prodigies, the Mausoleum had suddenly opened up, and a comet had appeared in the sky, he assigned the former omen to Junia Calvina, since she was from the family of Augustus, and the latter omen to the king of the Parthians, who had long hair. Even at the point of death he joked, saying, 'Woe is me! I think I am becoming a god'" (*ac ne in metu quidem ac periculo mortis extremo abstinuit iocis. nam cum inter cetera prodigia Mausoleum derepente patuisset et stella crinita in caelo apparuisset, alterum ad Iuniam Calvinam e gente Augusti pertinere*

dicebat, alterum ad Parthorum regem qui capillatus esset; prima quoque morbi accessione, "vae," inquit, "puto deus fio," Suet. *Vesp.* 23.4).

23. Johnston 1995:364.

24. Johnston 1991:217.

25. Stewart 1982.

26. Johnston 1995:370.

27. Penzoldt 1952:3. See also Hickman 1938.

28. Cox and Gilbert [1986] 1990:xii.

29. Grider 1997:4–5. At the same time, the growth of a reading public with leisure time, and new methods for producing and distributing books, opened up a whole new market for the novel. See Clery 1995:5 ff.

30. The short story rather than the novel was the popular form not only for ghost stories but for other kinds of literature, as the magazine became a convenient outlet. Though serialization of full-length novels was also common, the magazine format was highly conducive to the short story. See Cox and Gilbert 1991:xi.

31. Ibid.: x.

32. See Leithauser 1987.

33. Brennan 1996:253–55.

34. Ibid.: 258.

35. Cox 1996:xi.

36. Jackson 1959:5.

37. See Hoppenstand and Browne 1987; and Hatlen 1991:88 ff.

38. Sullivan 1978:134.

39. Ibid.: 71.

BIBLIOGRAPHY

Aarne, A., and S. Thompson. 1961. *The Types of the Folktale: A Classification and Bibliography*. Folklore Fellows Communications, no. 184. Helsinki: Academia Scientiarum Fennica.

Abbot, Frank Frost, and Allan Chester Johnson. 1926. *Municipal Administration in the Roman Empire*. Princeton: Princeton University Press.

Anderson, Graham. 1976a. *Studies in Lucian's Comic Fiction*. Leiden: E. J. Brill.

————. 1976b. *Lucian: Theme and Variation in the Second Sophistic*. Leiden: E. J. Brill.

Anderson, Warren. 1970. *Theophrastus: The Character Sketches*. [Kent, Ohio:] The Kent State University Press.

Anson, Jay. 1977. *The Amityville Horror*. Englewood Cliffs, N.J.: Prentice-Hall.

Asimov, Isaac, and Frederic Pohl. [1991] 1993. "Legal Rites." In *Ghosts,* edited by Marvin Kaye, 28–54. New York: Garland.

Austin, R. G. 1964. *P. Vergili Maronis Aeneidos Liber Secundus*. Oxford: Clarendon.

Ausubel, Nathan. [1948] 1977. *A Treasury of Jewish Folklore*. New York: Crown.

Baker, Ronald L. 1982. *Hoosier Folk Legends*. Bloomington: Indiana University Press.

Banti, Luisa. 1930. "Una scena della 'Mostellaria'." *Studi Italiani di filologia classica* 8: 67–82.

Bascom, William. 1965. "The Forms of Folklore: Prose Narratives." *Journal of American Folklore* 78.307: 3–20.

Baughman, Ernest W. 1945. "The Fatal Initiation." *Hoosier Folklore Bulletin* 4.3: 49–55.

————. 1966. *Type and Motif-Index of the Folktales of England and North America*. Indiana Folklore Series, no. 20. The Hague: Mouton.

Beare, W. 1950. *The Roman Stage*. London: Methuen.

Bennett, Gillian, and Paul Smith. 1993. *Contemporary Legend: A Folklore Bibliography*. New York and London: Garland.

Bettini, Maurizio. 1981. *Plauto Mostellaria Persa*. Milan: Arnoldo Mondadori.

Bierce, Ambrose. 1941. *The Devil's Dictionary*. Cleveland and New York: World Publishing Company.

Bleiler, E. F. 1966. *The Castle of Otranto by Horace Walpole, Vathek by William Beckford, The Vampyre by John Polidori: Three Gothic Novels, and a Fragment of a Novel by Lord Byron*. New York: Dover.

Blum, Richard, and Eva Blum. 1970. *The Dangerous Hour: The Lore of Crisis and Mystery in Rural Greece*. London: Chatto & Windus.

Bonner, Campbell. 1932. "Demons of the Baths." In *Studies Presented to F.Ll. Griffith*, edited by S.R.K. Glanville, 203–8. London: Egypt Exploration Society.

Botsford, George Willis. 1909. *The Roman Assemblies from Their Origin to the End of the Republic*. New York: Macmillan.

Bowersock, G. W. 1969. *Greek Sophists in the Roman Empire*. Oxford: Clarendon.

Braginton, Mary V. 1933. *The Supernatural in Seneca's Tragedies*. Menasha, Wis.: George Banta.

Brennan, Joseph Payne. 1996. "Can the Supernatural Story Survive?" In *American Supernatural Fiction from Edith Wharton to the Weird Tales Writers*, edited by Douglas Robillard, 253–60. New York: Garland.

Briggs, Julia. 1977. *Night Visitors: The Rise and Fall of the English Ghost Story*. London: Faber and Faber Limited.

Brown, P. G. McC. 1995. "Aeschinus at the Door: Terence *Adelphoe* 632–43 and the Traditions of Greco-Roman Comedy." *Papers of the Leeds International Latin Seminar* 8: 71–89.

Brown, Theo. 1979. *The Fate of the Dead*. Cambridge: D. S. Brewer Ltd.; Totowa, N.J.: Rowman and Littlefield for the Folklore Society.

Browne, Thomas. *Hydriotaphia*. [1658] 1977. New York: Arno.

Bruce, J. Douglas. 1913. "Human Automata in Classical Tradition and Mediaeval Romance." *Modern Philology* 10: 511–26.

Brunvand, Jan Harold. 1981. *The Vanishing Hitchhiker: American Urban Legends and Their Meanings*. New York: W. W. Norton.

Burkert, Walter. 1972. *Lore and Science in Ancient Pythagoreanism*. Translated by Edwin L. Minar, Jr. Cambridge, Mass.: Harvard University Press.

———. 1983. *Homo Necans: The Anthropology of Ancient Greek Sacrificial Ritual and Myth*. Translated by Peter Bing. Berkeley and Los Angeles: University of California Press.

———. 1985. *Greek Religion*. Translated by John Raffan. Cambridge, Mass.: Harvard University Press.

Carrington, Hereward, and Nandor Fodor. 1951. *Haunted People: Story of the Poltergeist Down the Centuries*. New York: E. P. Dutton.

Carskadan, Mary A., ed. 1993. *Encyclopedia of Sleep and Dreaming*. New York: Macmillan.

Christiansen, Reidar. 1958. *The Migratory Legends*. Folklore Fellows Communications, no. 175. Helsinki: Academia Scientiarum Fennica.

Clery, E. J. 1995. *The Rise of Supernatural Fiction, 1762–1800*. Cambridge: Cambridge University Press.

Collart, Jean. 1970. *T. Maccius Plautus Mostellaria*. Paris: Presses universitaires de France.

Collison-Morley, Lacy. [1912] 1968. *Greek and Roman Ghost Stories*. Chicago: Argonaut.

Cox, Michael. 1996. *The Oxford Book of Twentieth-Century Ghost Stories*. Oxford: Oxford University Press.

Cox, Michael, and R. A. Gilbert. [1986] 1990. *The Oxford Book of English Ghost Stories*. Oxford: Oxford University Press.

———. 1991. *Victorian Ghost Stories: An Oxford Anthology*. Oxford: Oxford University Press.

Cumont, Franz. [1922] 1923. *After Life in Roman Paganism*. New Haven, Conn.: Yale University Press.

———. 1949. *Lux Perpetua*. Paris: Librairie Orientaliste Paul Geuthner.

Daly, Robert. 1990. "Liminality and Fiction in Cooper, Hawthorne, Cather, and Fitzgerald." In *Victor Turner and the Construction of Cultural Criticism*, edited by Kathleen M. Ashley, 70–85. Bloomington and Indianapolis: Indiana University Press.

Davis, Wade. 1985. *The Serpent and the Rainbow*. New York: Simon and Schuster.

Dégh, Linda, ed. 1980. *Indiana Folklore: A Reader*. Bloomington: Indiana University Press.

Dégh, Linda, and Andrew Vázsonyi. 1976. "Legend and Belief." In *Folklore Genres*, edited by Dan Ben-Amos, 93–123. Austin: University of Texas Press.

Dingwall, E. J. 1930. *Ghosts and Spirits in the Ancient World*. London: Kegan Paul, Trench, Trubner & Co., Ltd.

Dodds, E. R. 1951. *The Greeks and the Irrational*. Berkeley and Los Angeles: University of California Press.

———. 1973. "Supernormal Phenomena in Classical Antiquity." In *The Ancient Concept of Progress and Other Essays on Greek Literature and Belief*, 156–210. Oxford: Clarendon.

Dorsch, T. S., ed. [1955] 1983. *Julius Caesar*. The Arden Edition of the Works of William Shakespeare. London and New York: Methuen.

Drexler, J. 1894–97. "Meridianus daemon." In *Ausfürliches Lexikon der griechischen und römischen Mythologie*, vol. 2, edited by W. H. Roscher, 2832–36. Leipzig: B. G. Teubner.

Duckworth, George E. 1952. *The Nature of Roman Comedy: A Study in Popular Entertainment*. Princeton: Princeton University Press.

Dundes, Alan. 1965. "The Study of Folklore in Literature and Culture: Identification and Interpretation." *Journal of American Folklore* 78.308: 136–42.

———. 1971. "On the Psychology of Legend." In *American Folk Legend: A Symposium*, edited by Wayland D. Hand, 21–36. Berkeley and Los Angeles: University of California Press.

———. 1993. "Series Editor's Preface." In *Contemporary Legend: A Folklore Bibliography*, edited by Gillian Bennett and Paul Smith, ix–xiii. New York and London: Garland.

Dyck, Andrew R. 1996. *A Commentary on Cicero, De officiis*. Ann Arbor: University of Michigan Press.

Edmunds, Lowell. 1984. "Thucydides on Monosandalism (3.22.2)." In *Studies Pre-*

sented to Sterling Dow on his Eightieth Birthday. *Greek, Roman, and Byzantine Monographs,* no. 10: 71–75. Durham, N.C.: Duke University.

Ellis, Bill. 1983. "*De Legendis Urbis:* Modern Legends in Ancient Rome." *Journal of American Folklore* 96: 200–208.

————. 1993. "Adolescent Legend-Tripping." *Psychology Today* 17.8: 68–69.

Enright, D. J., ed. 1983. *The Oxford Book of Death.* Oxford: Oxford University Press.

————. 1994. *The Oxford Book of the Supernatural.* Oxford: Oxford University Press.

Faraone, Christopher A. 1991a. "The Agonistic Context of Early Greek Binding Spells." In *Magika Hiera: Ancient Greek Magic and Religion,* edited by Christopher A. Faraone and Dirk Obbink, 3–32. Oxford: Oxford University Press.

————. 1991b. "Binding and Burying the Forces of Evil: The Defensive Use of 'Voodoo Dolls' in Ancient Greece." *Classical Antiquity* 10.2: 165–220.

Fenton, Daniel H. 1921. *Repetition of Thought in Plautus.* New Haven, Conn.: n.p.

Finucane, R. C. 1982. *Appearances of the Dead: A Cultural History of Ghosts.* London: Junction Books.

Fontenrose, Joseph. 1959. *Python: A Study of Delphic Myth and Its Origins.* Berkeley and Los Angeles: University of California Press.

————. [1978] 1981. *The Delphic Oracle.* Berkeley, Los Angeles, London: University of California Press.

Frank, Frederick S., and Anthony Magistrale. 1997. *The Poe Encyclopedia.* Westport, Conn.: Greenwood.

Frazer, J. G. [1897] 1913. *Pausanias' Description of Greece.* 6 vols. London: Macmillan.

————. 1929. *Publii Ovidii Nasonis Fastorum Libri Sex.* 5 vols. London: Macmillan.

————. 1933. *The Fear of the Dead in Primitive Religion.* 3 vols. London: Macmillan.

Frier, Bruce W. 1980. *Landlords and Tenants in Imperial Rome.* Princeton: Princeton University Press.

Furneaux, Henry. [1896] 1968. *The Annals of Tacitus.* Vol. 1: Books 1–6. 2d ed. Oxford: Clarendon.

Gager, John G., ed. 1992. *Curse Tablets and Binding Spells from the Ancient World.* New York and Oxford: Oxford University Press.

Garland, Robert. 1985. *The Greek Way of Death.* Ithaca, N.Y.: Cornell University Press.

Garton, Charles. 1972. *Personal Aspects of the Roman Theatre.* Toronto: A. M. Hakkert.

Gaster, Theodor H. [1969] 1981. *Myth, Legend, and Custom in the Old Testament.* 2 vols. Gloucester, Mass.: Peter Smith.

Gerould, Gordon Hall. 1908. *The Grateful Dead.* Publications of the Folklore Society, no. 60. London: David Nutt.

Giannini, Alexander. 1965. *Paradoxographorum graecorum reliquiae.* Milan: Istituto editoriale italiano.

Gildersleeve, B. L., and Gonzalez Lodge. [1867] 1986. *Gildersleeve's Latin Grammar.* London: Macmillan.

Goodwin, Leslie. 1994. "Spooky Dealings." *News and Observer,* Raleigh, N.C., October 30: 1D.

Grider, Sylvia. 1997. "The Haunted House in Literature, Legend, and American Popular Culture: A Paper in Honor of the 100th Anniversary of the Publication of Bram Stoker's *Dracula.*" Presented at the 1997 annual meeting of the International Society for Contemporary Legend Research, May 21–24, 1997. 24 pages.

Grimal, Pierre. [1951] 1986. *The Dictionary of Classical Mythology.* Translated by A. R. Maxwell-Hyslop. Oxford: Blackwell Reference.

Guiley, Rosemary Ellen. 1992. *The Encyclopedia of Ghosts and Spirits.* New York: Facts on File.

Gulick, Charles Burton. 1896. "Omens and Augury in Plautus." *Harvard Studies in Classical Philology* 7: 235–47.

Haining, Peter. 1982. *A Dictionary of Ghosts.* London: Robert Hale.

Halliday, W. R. [1913] 1967. *Greek Divination: A Study of Its Methods and Principles.* Chicago: Argonaut.

———. 1930. "'The Superstitious Man' of Theophrastus." *Folk-lore* 41: 121–53.

Halpert, Herbert. 1971. "Definition and Variation in Folk Legend." In *American Folk Legend: A Symposium,* edited by Wayland D. Hand, 47–54. Berkeley and Los Angeles: University of California Press.

Hansen, William F. 1980. "An Ancient Greek Ghost Story." In *Folklore on Two Continents: Essays in Honor of Linda Dégh,* edited by Nikolai Burlakoff and Carl Lindahl, 71–77. Bloomington: Trickster Press.

———. 1988. "Folklore." In *Civilization of the Ancient Mediterranean: Greece and Rome,* vol. 2, edited by Michael Grant and Rachel Kitzinger, 1121–30. New York: Charles Scribner's Sons.

———. 1989. "Contextualizing the Story of Philinnion." *Midwestern Folklore* 15: 101–8.

———. 1996. *Phlegon of Tralles' Book of Marvels.* Exeter: University of Exeter Press.

Hastings, James, ed. 1919. *Encyclopedia of Religion and Ethics.* New York: Charles Scribner's Sons.

Hatlen, Burton. 1991. "Good and Evil in Stephen King's *The Shining.*" In *The Shining Reader,* edited by Anthony Magistrale, 81–104. Mercer Island, Wash.: Starmont House.

Hearn, Michael Patrick. 1976. *The Annotated Christmas Carol: A Christmas Carol by Charles Dickens.* New York: Clarkson N. Potter.

Heubeck, Alfred and Arie Hoekstra. [1989] 1990. *A Commentary on Homer's Odyssey.* Vol. 2: Books 9–16. Oxford: Clarendon.

Hickman, Ruby Mildred. 1938. *Ghostly Etiquette on the Classical Stage.* Cedar Rapids, Iowa: Torch Press.

Hill, George Birkbeck, ed. 1891. *Boswell's Life of Johnson.* 6 vols. New York and London: Harper & Brothers.

Hopkins, Keith. 1983. *Death and Renewal*. Sociological Studies in Roman History, vol. 2. Cambridge: Cambridge University Press.

Hoppenstand, Gary, and Ray B. Browne. 1987. *The Gothic World of Stephen King: Landscape of Nightmares*. Bowling Green, Ohio: Bowling Green State University Popular Press.

Jackson, Shirley. 1959. *The Haunting of Hill House*. New York: Fawcett Popular Library.

Jaffé, Aniela. 1979. *Apparitions: An Archetypal Approach to Death Dreams and Ghosts*. Irving, Tex.: Spring Publications.

James, Henry. 1992. *The Turn of the Screw and Other Stories*. Edited by T. J. Lustig. Oxford: Oxford University Press.

James, M. R. 1987. "Some Remarks on Ghost Stories." In *"Casting the Runes" and Other Ghost Stories,* edited by Michael Cox, 342–49. Oxford: Oxford University Press.

Jebb, R. C. 1909. *The Characters of Theophrastus*. London: Macmillan.

Jenkins, Harold, ed. [1982] 1984. *Hamlet*. The Arden Edition of the Works of William Shakespeare. London and New York: Methuen.

Jobbé-Duval, Émile. 1924. *Les Morts malfaisants: "Larvae, lemures" d'après le droit et les croyances populaires des romains*. Paris: Librarie du Recueil Sirey.

Johnston, Sarah Iles. 1990. *Hekate Soteira*. Atlanta, Georgia: Scholars Press.

———. 1991. "Crossroads." *Zeitschrift für Papyrologie und Epigraphik* 88: 217–24.

———. 1994. "Introduction." In "Exploring the Shadows: Ancient Literature and the Supernatural." *Helios* 21.2: 99–105.

———. 1995. "Defining the Dreadful: Remarks on the Greek Child-Killing Demon." In *Ancient Magic and Ritual Power,* edited by Marvin Meyer and Paul Mirecki, 361–87. Religions in the Greco-Roman World, vol. 129. Leiden: E. J. Brill.

Jones, C. P. 1986. *Culture and Society in Lucian*. Cambridge, Mass.: Harvard University Press.

Jones, Louis C. 1959. *Things That Go Bump in the Night*. New York: Hill and Wang.

Joshi, S. T. 1990. *The Weird Tale*. Austin: University of Texas Press.

Keller, Otto, ed. 1877. *Rerum naturalium scriptores graeci minores*. Vol. 1. Leipzig: Teubner.

Kemper, J.A.R. 1993. "How Ill This Taper Burns! Spirits, Revenge, Philosophers, and the Demonic Power of Rhetoric." *File: A Literary Journal* 2.4: 9–27.

Kenney, E. J., and W. V. Clausen. 1982. *The Cambridge History of Classical Literature,* vol. 2, part 4, "The Early Principate." Cambridge: Cambridge University Press.

Klotsche, Ernest Heinrich. 1918. "The Supernatural in the Tragedies of Euripides as Illustrated in Prayers, Curses, Oaths, Oracles, Prophecies, Dreams, and Visions." *The University Studies of the University of Nebraska* 18: 55–106.

Knight, W. F. Jackson. 1970. *Elysion: On Ancient Greek and Roman Beliefs Concerning a Life After Death*. New York: Barnes & Noble.

Krappe, Alexander H. 1943. "Spirit-Sighted Animals." *Folk-lore* 54: 391–401.

Krauss, Franklin Brunell. 1930. *An Interpretation of the Omens, Portents, and Prodigies Recorded by Livy, Tacitus, and Suetonius*. Philadelphia: [University of Pennsylvania].

Kytzler, Bernhard. 1989. *Geister, Gräber und Gespenster: Antike Spukgeschichten*. Leipzig: Teubner.

Lang, Andrew. 1885. "The Comparative Study of Ghost Stories." *Nineteenth Century* 17: 623–32.

———. 1896. *Cock-Lane and Common Sense*. London, New York, and Bombay: Longmans, Green.

———. [1897] 1970. *The Book of Dreams and Ghosts*. New York: AMS Press.

Larson, Jennifer. 1995. *Greek Heroine Cults*. Madison: University of Wisconsin Press.

Lateiner, Donald. 1990. "Deceptions and Delusions in Herodotus." *Classical Antiquity* 9.2: 230–46.

Lattimore, Richmond. [1942] 1962. *Themes in Greek and Latin Epitaphs*. Urbana: University of Illinois Press.

Lawson, John Cuthbert. 1964. *Modern Greek Folklore and Ancient Greek Religion*. Reprint. New York: University Books.

Leithauser, Brad. 1987. "Dead Forms: The Ghost Story Today." *New Criterion* 6.4: 29–37.

Lilja, Saara. 1978. "Descriptions of Human Appearance in Pliny's Letters." *Arctos* 12: 55–62.

Liljeblad, Sven. 1927. *Die Tobiasgeschichte und andere Märchen mit toten Helfern*. Lund: A.-B. Ph. Lindstedts Univ.-Bokhandel.

Lloyd-Jones, Hugh. 1982. *Blood for the Ghosts: Classical Influences in the Nineteenth and Twentieth Centuries*. London: Duckworth.

Lovecraft, Howard Phillips. [1945] 1973. *Supernatural Horror in Literature*. New York: Dover.

Luck, Georg. [1985] 1992. *Arcana Mundi: Magic and the Occult in the Greek and Roman Worlds*. Baltimore and London: The Johns Hopkins University Press.

Lüthi, Max. 1976. "Aspects of the *Märchen* and the Legend." In *Folklore Genres*, edited by Dan Ben-Amos, 17–33. Austin: University of Texas Press.

Mabbot, Thomas Ollive. 1969. *Collected Works of Edgar Allan Poe*. Vol. 1. Cambridge, Mass.: The Belknap Press of Harvard University Press.

McCartney, Eugene S. 1947. "A Bibliography of Collections of Greek and Roman Folklore." *Classical Weekly* 40.13: 99–101.

Machen, Arthur. [1948] 1973. *Tales of Horror and the Supernatural*. Vol. 2. New York: Pinnacle.

MacKenzie, Andrew. 1971. *Apparitions and Ghosts*. London: Arthur Barker Limited.

Matheson, Richard. 1971. *Hell House*. New York: Viking.

Merrill, Elmer Truesdell. [1903] 1911. *Selected Letters of the Younger Pliny*. London: Macmillan.

Merrill, Frank R. 1972. *Titi Macci Plauti Mostellaria*. New York: St. Martin's Press.

Messent, Peter B., ed. 1981. *Literature of the Occult: A Collection of Critical Essays.* Englewood Cliffs, N.J.: Prentice-Hall.

Mommsen, Theodor, ed. 1985. *The Digest of Justinian.* Vol. 2. English translation edited by Alan Watson. Philadelphia: University of Pennsylvania Press.

Montell, William Lynwood. 1975. *Ghosts along the Cumberland: Deathlore in the Kentucky Foothills.* Knoxville: University of Tennessee Press.

Moore, Clifford Herschel. 1963. *Ancient Beliefs in the Immortality of the Soul.* New York: Cooper Square.

Morris, E. P. [1880] 1881. *The Mostellaria of Plautus.* Boston: John Allyn.

Myers, F.W.H. 1961. *Human Personality and Its Survival of Bodily Death.* New Hyde Park, N.Y.: University Books.

Nardi, Enzo. 1960. *Case "infestate da spiriti" e diritto Romano e moderno.* Milan: Dott. A. Giuffrè.

———. 1975–76a. "Case infestate nella letteratura antica." *Rendiconti dell' Accademia delle Scienze dell' Istituto di Bologna* 64: 87–98.

———. 1975–76b. "Il problema giuridico delle case infestate." *Rendiconti dell' Accademia delle Scienze dell' Istituto di Bologna* 64: 99–109.

Nilsson, Martin P. [1925] 1949. *A History of Greek Religion.* 2d ed. Translated by F. J. Fielden. Oxford: Clarendon.

———. [1940] 1961. *Greek Folk Religion.* New York: Columbia University Press.

O'Hara, James J. 1990. *Death and the Optimistic Prophecy in Vergil's Aeneid.* Princeton: Princeton University Press.

Olrik, Axel. [1921] 1992. *Principles for Oral Narrative Research.* Bloomington: Indiana University Press.

Opie, Iona, and Moira Tatem, ed. 1989. *A Dictionary of Superstitions.* Oxford: Oxford University Press.

Palmer, Christopher, ed. 1988. *The Collected Arthur Machen.* London: Duckworth.

Parker, Robert. 1983. *Miasma: Pollution and Purification in Early Greek Religion.* Oxford: Clarendon.

Pasquali, G. 1929. "Leggendo." *Studi Italiani di Filologia Classica* 7: 305–23.

Pease, Arthur Stanley, ed. 1920. "M. Tulli Ciceronis De Divinatione Liber Primus." *University of Illinois Studies in Language and Literature* 6.2–3: 1–338.

Pentikäinen, Juha. 1968. *The Nordic Dead-Child Tradition.* Folklore Fellows Communications, no. 202. Helsinki: Academia Scientiarum Fennica.

Penzoldt, Peter. 1952. *The Supernatural in Fiction.* London: Peter Nevill.

Perna, Raffaele. 1955. *L'originalità di Plauto.* Bari.

Pfaff, Richard William. 1980. *Montague Rhodes James.* London: Scolar Press.

Phillips, C. Robert III. 1992. "Roman Religion and Literary Studies of Ovid's *Fasti.*" *Arethusa* 25: 55–80.

Porter, J. R. 1981. "Ghosts in the Old Testament and the Ancient Near East." In *The Folklore of Ghosts,* edited by Hilda R. Ellis Davidson and W.M.S. Russell, 215–38. Cambridge: D. S. Brewer for the Folklore Society.

Prichard, Constantine E., and Edward R. Bernard. 1896. *Selected Letters of Pliny.* Oxford: Clarendon.

Radermacher, L. 1979. "Aus Lucians Lügenfreund." In *Festschrift Theodor Gomperz dargebracht zum siebzigsten Geburtstage am 29. März 1902,* edited by Moritz Schwind, 197–207. Reprint. Vienna: Scientia Verlag Aalen.

Rohde, Erwin. 1925. *Psyche: The Cult of Souls and Belief in Immortality Among the Greeks.* London: Kegan Paul, Trench, Trubner.

Röhrich, Lutz. 1981. "Dankbarer Toter." In *Enzyklopädie des Märchens* 3: 306–22. Berlin and New York: Walter de Gruyter.

Römer, Franz. 1987. "Vom Spuk zur Politik: Der Gespensterbrief des Jüngeren Plinius." *Wiener humanistische Blätter* 29: 26–36.

Rose, H. J. 1959. *A Handbook of Greek Mythology.* New York: E. P. Dutton.

Russell, Claire. 1981. "The Environment of Ghosts." In *The Folklore of Ghosts,* edited by Hilda R. Ellis Davidson and W.M.S. Russell, 109–37. Cambridge: D. S. Brewer for the Folklore Society.

Russell, W.M.S. 1981. "Greek and Roman Ghosts." In *The Folklore of Ghosts,* edited by Hilda R. Ellis Davidson and W.M.S. Russell, 193–213. Cambridge: D. S. Brewer for the Folklore Society.

Rust, Richard Dilworth. 1988. "Liminality in *The Turn of the Screw.*" *Studies in Short Fiction* 25.4: 441–46.

Sarkissian, Gisèle. 1985. "Ghosts in Tales of the Fantastic." In *Mythes, croyances et religions dans le monde Anglo Saxon,* 3: 155–63. Avignon: Université d'Avignon.

Scarborough, Dorothy. [1917] 1967. *The Supernatural in Modern English Fiction.* New York: Octagon.

Schmidt, Bernhard. 1871. *Das Volksleben der Neugriechen und das hellenische Alterthum.* Erster Theil. Leipzig: B. G. Teubner.

Schwartz, Jacques. 1965. *Biographie de Lucien de Samosate.* Collection Latomus, vol. 83. Bruxelles: Latomus.

———. 1969. "Le Fantôme de l'Académie." In *Hommages à Marcel Renard,* vol. 1, edited by Jacqueline Bibauw, 671–76. Brussels: Latomus, Revue d'Etudes Latines.

Scobie, Alex. 1978. "Strigiform Witches in Roman and Other Cultures." *Fabula* 19: 74–101.

———. 1983. *Apuleius and Folklore.* London: The Folklore Society.

Scullard, H. H. 1981. *Festivals and Ceremonies of the Roman Republic.* Ithaca, N.Y.: Cornell University Press.

Segal, Charles. 1990. *Lucretius on Death and Anxiety.* Princeton: Princeton University Press.

Segal, Erich. 1987. *Roman Laughter: The Comedy of Plautus.* 2d ed. New York and Oxford: Oxford University Press.

Shain, Andrew. 1994. "Ghost Story Helps Sell S.C. Real Estate." *The News & Observer,* Raleigh, N.C., November 25: 26A.

Shelley, Mary. 1965. *Frankenstein, Or, The Modern Prometheus.* Reprint. New York: Signet.

Sherwin-White, A. N. [1966] 1985. *The Letters of Pliny: A Historical and Social Commentary.* Oxford: Clarendon.

Shorey, Paul, and Gordon J. Laing. [1919] 1960. *Horace: Odes and Epodes.* Pittsburgh: University of Pittsburgh Press.

Shrimpton, Gordon. 1980. "The Persian Cavalry at Marathon." *Phoenix* 34: 20–37.

Smith, Kirby F. 1894. "An Historical Study of the Werwolf in Literature." *Publications of the Modern Language Association of America* 9.1: 1–42.

Solomon, Jack, and Olivia Solomon. 1981. *Ghosts and Goosebumps: Ghost Stories, Tall Tales, and Superstitions from Alabama.* University: University of Alabama Press.

Sonnenschein, Edward A. 1907. *T. Macci Plauti Mostellaria.* Oxford: Clarendon.

Spencer, John, and Anne Spencer. 1992. *The Encyclopedia of Ghosts and Spirits.* London: Headline.

Stanford, W. B. 1940. "Ghosts and Apparitions in Homer, Aeschylus, and Shakespeare." *Hermathena* 56: 84–92.

———. 1955. *The Odyssey of Homer.* Vol. 1 (Books I–XII). London: Macmillan.

Stewart, Susan. 1982. "The Epistemology of the Horror Story." *Journal of American Folklore* 95: 33–50.

Strubbe, J.H.M. 1991. "Cursed Be He That Moves My Bones." In *Magika Hiera: Ancient Greek Magic and Religion,* edited by Christopher A. Faraone and Dirk Obbink, 33–59. Oxford: Oxford University Press.

Sturtevant, Edgar H. 1925. *T. Macci Plauti Mostellaria.* New Haven, Conn.: Yale University Press.

Sullivan, Jack. 1978. *Elegant Nightmares: The English Ghost Story from Le Fanu to Blackwood.* Athens: Ohio University Press.

———, ed. 1986. *The Penguin Encyclopedia of Horror and the Supernatural.* New York: Viking.

Sumwalt, Ann. 1995. "Tell It Like It Is." *Los Angeles Times,* Los Angeles, Calif., April 2: 1K.

Sussman, Lewis A. 1987. *The Major Declamations Ascribed to Quintilian. Studien zur klassischen Philologie.* Band 27. Frankfurt: Verlag Peter Lang.

Sutton, Dana F. 1993. *Ancient Comedy: The War of the Generations.* New York: Twayne.

Syme, Ronald. 1958. *Tacitus.* Oxford: Clarendon.

Terzaghi, Nicola. 1929. *T. Maccio Plauto La Mostellaria.* Torino: Paravia.

Thompson, Stith. 1955–58. *Motif-Index of Folk-Literature.* 6 vols. Bloomington: Indiana University Press.

Toynbee, J.M.C. 1948. "Beasts and Their Names in the Roman Empire." *Papers of the British School at Rome* 16: 24–37.

———. 1971. *Death and Burial in the Roman World.* New York: Cornell University Press.

Tripp, Edward. [1970] 1974. *The Meridian Handbook of Classical Mythology.* New York: Meridian.

Tyrrell, G.H.M. [1953] 1970. *Apparitions.* New York: Collier.

Ussher, R. G. 1960. *The Characters of Theophrastus.* London: Macmillan.

Ussing, Johan Louis. 1972. *Commentarius in Plauti Comoedias*. Reprint. Hildesheim: G. Olms.

Utley, Francis Lee. 1976. "Oral Genres as a Bridge to Written Literature." In *Folklore Genres*, edited by Dan Ben-Amos, 4–15. Austin: University of Texas Press.

Van Gennep, Arnold. 1960. *The Rites of Passage*. Translated by Monika B. Vizedom and Gabrielle L. Caffee. Chicago: University of Chicago Press.

Van Lieshout, R.G.A. 1980. *Greeks on Dreams*. Utrecht: Hes.

Vermeule, Emily. 1979. *Aspects of Death in Early Greek Art and Poetry*. Berkeley and Los Angeles: University of California Press.

Virtanen, Leea. 1990. *"That Must Have Been ESP!" An Examination of Psychic Experiences*. Bloomington and Indianapolis: Indiana University Press.

Voisin, Jean-Louis. 1984. "Les Romains, chasseurs de têtes." In *Du châtiment dans la cité: Supplices corporels et peine de mort dans le monde antique*, 241–93. Rome: Ecole Française.

Warmington, E. H. 1961. *Remains of Old Latin*. Vol. 2. Loeb Classical Library. Cambridge, Mass.: Harvard University Press.

Waszink, J. H., ed. 1947. *Quinti Septimi Florentis Tertulliani De anima*. Amsterdam: J. M. Meulenhoff.

Wendland, Paul. 1911. "Antike Geister- und Gespenstergeschichten." In *Festschrift zur Jahrhundertfeier der Universität zu Breslau, im Namen der schlesischen Gesellschaft für Volkskunde*, edited by Theodor Siebs, 33–55. Breslau: Kommissionsverlag von M. & H. Marcus.

Wharton, Edith. 1937. *Ghosts*. New York and London: D. Appleton-Century.

Whitmore, C. E. 1915. *The Supernatural in Tragedy*. Cambridge, Mass.: Harvard University Press.

Wieand, Helen E. 1920. *Deception in Plautus: A Study in the Technique of Roman Comedy*. Boston: Richard G. Badger.

Wilde, Oscar. 1906. *The Canterville Ghost*. Boston and London: John W. Luce.

Wilson, Colin. 1981. *Poltergeist! A Study in Destructive Haunting*. London: New English Library.

Winkler, Jack. 1980. "Lollianos and the Desperadoes." *Journal of Hellenic Studies* 100: 155–81.

Wise, Herbert A., and Phyllis Fraser. 1944. *Great Tales of Terror and the Supernatural*. New York: Modern Library.

Wright, John. 1974. *Dancing in Chains: The Stylistic Unity of the Comoedia Palliata*. Rome: American Academy in Rome.

Zanker, Paul. 1995. *The Mask of Socrates*. Translated by Alan Shapiro. Berkeley and Los Angeles: University of California Press.

Ziegler, Norma E. 1982. "Dreams in Plautine Comedy." Master's thesis, University of North Carolina, Chapel Hill.

GENERAL INDEX